FROM AMERICA TO UNITED STATES

Frontispiece: The liner AMERICA — the symbol and flagship of the American merchant marine in 1940 — and Hull No 1 of the United States Maritime Commission's shipbuilding programme.

L. A. SAWYER and W. H. MITCHELL

FROM AMERICA TO UNITED STATES

In Four Parts:

The History of the Merchant Ship types built in the United States of America under the Long-Range Programme of the Maritime Commission

— PART ONE —

World Ship Society, Kendal LA9 7LT
1979

By the same authors (from other publishing houses)

BRITISH STANDARD SHIPS OF WORLD WAR I

EMPIRE SHIPS OF WORLD WAR II

THE OCEANS, THE FORTS AND THE PARKS

American Standard Ships Series — companion volumes

THE LIBERTY SHIPS

VICTORY SHIPS AND TANKERS

THE CUNARD LINE — A POSTWAR HISTORY

TANKERS

CRUISING SHIPS

Printed by **Gibbons Barford Print** Wolverhampton

ISBN 0 905617 08 8

Contents

Introduction

When the United States of America entered World War II in December 1941 their shipyards commenced an immense task of shipbuilding which resulted in the American Merchant Marine becoming the largest merchant fleet, by far, ever under one flag.

Indeed, after only two years, when the highest monthly delivery of over two million tons of U.S.–built shipping had been made in December 1943, the Maritime Commission — the body appointed to rebuild the United States Merchant Marine — was able to turn its capabilities to the production of a variety of ship types for the armed forces.

About ten shipyards in the United States were capable of building ocean-going ships in 1937 but, by the end of 1943, some eighty yards were building for the Commission, employing over 700,000 personnel in yards on the Atlantic coast, the Pacific coast, the Gulf area and the Great Lakes.

In 1938 the newly-formed Maritime Commission, under the Merchant Marine Act of 1936, commenced rebuilding the United States merchant fleet with a programme of fifty ships a year for the ensuing ten years. By the summer of 1939 this had been increased to a hundred a year, this number doubled in 1940 and, in 1941, doubled again to four hundred per year. Again, in 1942, on order from the President of the United States the rate was increased to eight hundred, rising to a thousand in 1943 — some 18 million tons of shipping in two years. Even then this was not the end, for in February 1942 the Maritime Commission was again directed to increase this to 24 million tons for the period.

Nearly 6,000 merchant ships were built, of which 45% were constructed on the West coast, 34% on the East coast, 19% in the Gulf area and 2% on the Great Lakes.

Much of the tonnage came from the 'emergency' programme which was in addition to the long-term programme and included over 2,700 "Liberty" type ships, over five hundred of its sophisticated successor, the "Victory" ship and over five hundred turbo-electric as well as other type tankers.

The Maritime Commission commenced its long-term programme with the liner *America* — Hull No 1, which was ordered in October 1937 and the last delivery was that of the liner *United States* in 1952. Between these ships lies the fascinating story of the building of a gigantic merchant fleet.

The sequence of details shown herein for each ship is Yard number, original name of ship, completion date (these details are printed in **bold** type) and then the history. The date shown is the date each hull was completed for commercial use. Many ships, however, were then immediately ordered for conversion for naval or military purposes. Their final completion for those roles and subsequent first voyage dates were, therefore, weeks and sometimes several months later. In some cases hulls were actually acquired prior to their completion for commercial use.

Some entries in the historical details indicate that certain ships were/are attached to the United States Navy (USN) and the group letter/number designation shown indicates the USN classification and type. The key to these designations will be found separately. Also, under history, a reference to "Reserve" status indicates the situation of a given vessel and a complete list of the different Reserve Fleet sites is also shown separately. An entry without change of name or change in status generally indicates that such vessel remained under Maritime Commission jurisdiction, although the exception to this concerns vessels completed for or acquired by commercial companies and which, generally, were given company nomenclature.

It will be noted that some vessels, subsequent to a casualty, have been declared as a constructive total loss; this fact is indicated by the abbreviation CTL.

Generally the scrapping dates shown indicate the commencement of the ship-breaking operation.

The notation I, II, III, etc in parenthesis after a ship's name indicates that it is the first, second, third, etc ship of that name within the scope of the four "Part" indices of this book.

The book covers the building of ships for the Maritime Commission, except tankers and those of the "emergency" classes — the Liberty ships and the Victory ships. Detailed volumes covering these exceptions, by the same authors, have already been published elsewhere and together with this publication present a comprehensive story of the seventeen years of shipbuilding by the United States Maritime Commission.

Also included is the complete list of USMC hull numbers and the types of vessels concerned. It includes those numbers allocated to tankers — left in for the sake of continuity — though this type of vessel has been listed in parenthesis. The "emergency" types of vessels were given a separate series of hull numbers.

No attempt has been made, generally, within this text, to give shipyard and shipowning company histories to date. Relevant details are, approximately, to the period dealt with by the subject matter.

The work is in four parts:

Part One	includes the s.s. *America,* the C1, C1–M and P types:
Part Two	includes the C2, R, C4 and C5 types:
Part Three	includes the C3, V and L6 types, plus the wood and concrete ships:
Part Four	includes the N5 and S types, post-war liners, the C3-S-DX1 prototype, miscellaneous ships and the numerical list of all USMC hull Nos with the appropriate Yard Nos and ship types.

The authors wish to acknowledge, with grateful thanks, the assistance given them, particularly by Lloyd's Register of Shipping; the Corporation of Lloyd's (Lloyd's of London); the Salvage Association, London; the United States Maritime Administration; the United States Navy; Ingalls Shipbuilding Corporation; Messrs John Cashman, John Freestone, David Littlejohn and Roger Jordan of London, and for various photographic services to Skyfotos Ltd; Wright & Logan; and to Messrs Tom Rayner, Roy Kittle, John Callis and Alex Duncan of Great Britain; Tom Ellsworth, Eric Johnson and Samuel Morison of the U.S.A.; Vic Young of New Zealand, and to all other persons who have contributed facts, information and aid.

Line drawings are by Nigel V. Robinson, except where otherwise acknowledged.

Cover design by Thomas A. Adams, with ideas by Michael Crowdy and the authors.

London and Southampton

February 1979

L. A. Sawyer
W. H. Mitchell

Glossary

ASROC	—	anti-submarine rocket
bhp	—	brake horsepower (the power developed by diesel machinery at the output flange [brake]).
bp	—	(length) between perpendiculars
CTL	—	constructive total loss (damaged beyond economic repair)
cyl	—	cylinder
Drone	—	anti-submarine helicopter (carrying remotely-controlled torpedoes)
FRAM I and FRAM II	—	Fleet rebuilding and modernisation (programmes)
grt	—	gross registered tons
hp	—	horsepower
ihp	—	indicated horsepower (the power developed in reciprocating machinery as measured by indicators on each cylinder)
LPG	—	liquefied petroleum gas
lwt	—	light weight type (anchors in lbs).
Marad	—	Maritime Administration
MSC	—	Military Sealift Command
MSTS	—	Military Sea Transportation Service (later Military Sealift Command)
oa	—	(length) overall
rpm	—	revolutions per minute
scantlings	—	the sizes of the component parts of a ship's structure, e.g. widths and thicknesses of frames, angles, plating, etc.
shp	—	shaft horsepower (the power developed by steam turbine machinery at the shaft)
tdw	—	tons, deadweight — the actual weight of cargo, fuel etc a ship is permitted to carry (in tons of 2240 lbs.)
USMC	—	United States Maritime Commission
USNS	—	United States Naval Ship
wl	—	(length) waterline
WPB	—	War Production Board
WSA	—	War Shipping Administration

Maritime Commission ship designations

These designations were divided into three groups of letters and numbers, each outlining the characteristics of the vessel.

In the first group a letter was used in conjunction with a number, the letter indicating the type of vessel, such as cargo, passenger, etc., and the number its approximate waterline length (see Table 1).

The middle (or second) group indicated, first by letters, the type of machinery whilst the number indicated the number of screws and the fact that the ship had accommodation for more than twelve passengers. If twelve or fewer passengers were carried the number was omitted, the letter "T" added (where necessary) to indicate twin screws (see Table 2).

It can be seen that there may be a length variation —for example a 'C2' in Table 1 — in the range of 400-450 feet, and thus it was necessary to have a design letter to fit a particular vessel. The third group, therefore, indicated the design letter allocated to a ship's hull, this letter remaining fixed regardless of any future change. Still within this third group, then, a number following the letter indicated the original arrangement of the particular design. This number could be varied to reflect changes of a major nature made internally or to the superstructure: thus number 1 was the original ship, number 2 the first modification, and so on.

In addition to this standard method of classifying Maritime Commission ships, special letters were used as a prefix to the first group for certain other constructions, such as 'E' for the emergency-programme Liberty ships, "V" for the Victory type ships, etc.

Table 1

Type of vessel . . . . Waterline length (in feet)

		1	2	3	4	5	6	7
C	Cargo — unlimited service (Under 100 pass.)	Under 400	400–450	450–500	500–550	—	—	—
P	Pass. — unlimited service (Over 100 pass.)	Under 500	500–600	600–700	700–800	800–900	900–1000	Over 1000
B	Barge	Under 100	100–150	150–200	200–250	250–300	—	—
L	Great Lakes (ore/grain)	Under 400	400–450	450–500	500–550	550–600	600–650	—
N	Coastwise cargo	Under 200	200–250	250–300	300–350	350–400	400–450	450–500
R	Refrigerated	Under 400	400–450	450–500	500–550	—	—	—
S	Special (see note below)	Under 200	200–300	300–400	400–500	500–600	600–700	—
T	Tanker (see note below)	Under 450	450–500	500–550	—	—	—	—
V	Towing vessels	Under 50	50–100	100–150	150–200	—	—	—

Note: The Special designation takes care of certain U.S. Navy vessels built by the USMC. Tankers have been included here as these vessels, with full type description, are listed — for continuity — in the complete USMC Hull No. List which will be shown in Part Four.

Table 2

Type of machinery	No. of propellers	Under 12 passengers	Over 12 passengers
Steam	Single	S	S1
Motor	Single	M	M1
Turbo-electric	Single	SE	SE1
Diesel-electric	Single	ME	ME1
Steam	Twin	ST	S2
Motor	Twin	MT	M2
Turbo-electric	Twin	SET	SE2
Diesel-electric	Twin	MET	ME2

U.S. Navy classification and types

The prefix "T" indicates operation of a vessel by the MSTS/MSC

ACV	=	Aircraft carrier, escort
AD	=	Destroyer tender
AE	=	Ammunition ship
AF	=	Refrigerated store ship
AG	=	Auxiliary (miscellaneous)
AGC	=	Amphibious force flagship (previously Combined Operations HQ ship)
AGM	=	Missile range instrumentation ship
AGP	=	Motor torpedo boat tender
AGS	=	Support ship to fleet ballistic missile programme
AGTR	=	Technical and scientific research ship
AH	=	Hospital ship
AK	=	Cargo ship
AKA	=	Attack cargo ship
AKS	=	General stores issue ship
AKV	=	Cargo ship and aircraft ferry
AO	=	Navy tanker/oiler
AP	=	Transport
APA	=	Attack transport
APC	=	Coastal transport
APD	=	High speed transport
APH	=	Transport fitted for the evacuation of wounded
APV	=	Transport and aircraft ferry
AR	=	Repair ship
ARC	=	Cable ship
ARG	=	Repair ship, internal combustion engines
ARH	=	Heavy hull repair ship
ARL	=	Repair ship, landing craft
ARV	=	Aircraft repair ship
AS	=	Submarine tender
AT	=	Tug
AV	=	Seaplane tender
AVG	=	Aircraft carrier, escort
AVP	=	Seaplane tender, small
AVS	=	Aviation supply ship
BAK	=	Cargo craneship
BAVG	=	Aircraft carrier, escort (British)
CVE	=	Aircraft carrier, escort
CVHA	=	Assault helicopter transport
CVHE	=	Escort helicopter carrier
CVU	=	Utility aircraft carrier
IX	=	Unclassified vessel
LCC	=	Amphibious command ship
LKA	=	Amphibious cargo ship
LPH	=	Amphibious assault ship
LST	=	Landing ship, tank
PF	=	Frigate
YCF	=	Car float
YD	=	Floating derrick
YFP	=	Floating power plant
YO	=	Fuel oil barge
YOG	=	Gasoline barge
YTB	=	Harbour tug, big

FROM AMERICA TO UNITED STATES

There are, basically, two kinds of ships. Ships of war and ships of peace. In time of peace each type plays its separate peaceful role, but in time of war the types combine to play a single role for to a maritime nation the merchant ship in time of war automatically becomes a complementary backing to the country's naval strength, either in continuing to serve the nation with its war requirements or to become an auxiliary to the naval forces.

In the United States the fact that a navy without a supporting merchant marine is handicapped, has been realised several times, leading to merchant marine legislation through Acts of Congress with the prime objective of strengthening the merchant ship fleet, both for peaceful operation and for war emergency.

Four such Acts have been passed up to World War II — in 1916, in 1920, 1928 and 1936. From two of the Acts — those of 1916 and 1936 — the story of the American wartime standard ships evolved and in commencing the story of these ships, as apart from the 'emergency' ships of World War II, it is interesting and perhaps even necessary to give some broad background to the standard ships of World War I.

THE EMERGENCY FLEET CORPORATION

It was in 1916, before the United States was at war, that the Shipping Act was passed, enabling the Government to create a department of the administration — the United States Shipping Board — to programme the building of more ships for both peacetime and time of war. Within the Act was a proviso that the Board be enabled to form a Corporation for the actual building of ships, these to be managed and administered by the Board. On 6 April 1917 the United States declared war on Germany and on 17 April the Emergency Fleet Corporation was formed.

To speed the production of ships, standard designs were used in many instances, parts of ships being constructed in ironworks, bridge-building and other engineering establishments and transported to the shipyard for assembly. The result of the immense effort through the Emergency Fleet Corporation was the building of some 1,500 vessels, the majority of which were tramp-type steamers. Many other smaller types of ships were also built and some 600, for speed of construction, were built of wood. The timber however, was so unseasoned that serious warping caused leakage to many hulls, sometimes before the ships had even been loaded. There were also more than 100 'Lakers' built on the Great Lakes, limited in their size to the Welland Canal locks. Under an international agreement there were also a number built in Japan.

By 1922 the frenzied shipbuilding programme was completed, the United States owning the second largest merchant fleet in the world. During the period 1917-1921, 2,493 merchant ships over 100 grt, totalling 10,355,912 grt had been built and on the Great Lakes 496 were constructed of 1,242,052 grt.

But the tramp ships that had been built were slow, only a few exceeding $10\frac{1}{2}$ knots, and they were found to be unsuitable for use in the post-war cargo liner trade with many financial losses. A good number were scrapped after only a year or so of service. Many others remained in government ownership, chartered out to operators under a miscellany of agreements, or swinging at their anchor chains in the rivers and backwaters of the United States. Some of these eventually found their way to the British flag early in World War II, being renamed with the familiar 'Empire' prefix of the Ministry of Shipping of that time (later Ministry of War Transport).

SHIPBUILDING IN THE EARLY 1920s

In the early 1920s many builders, faced with blank order books turned to civil construction, steelwork, bridges, buildings and the like and only the well established yards remained active to build ships.

There were however, a number of interesting ships built during the decade stretching through to the mid-1930s and these should be mentioned in this somewhat strange era of United States maritime history.

It is significant to note that no dry cargo ships were built during this period until the Newport News SB & DD Co turned out the ANGELINA and MANUELA (4,772 grt) in 1934. There were however, a number of passenger ships constructed for the protected coastwise services of the United States, the incentive to build made by the Acts of 1920 and 1928 which gave government authority to make construction loans and mortgage guarantees to private owners desiring new ships and although a number of operators in foreign trade used the low term charter rates of the US Shipping Board cargo steamers, a large number of interesting coastal passenger ships were built.

Practically all these were built in the 'big five' yards which remained in production throughout the inter-war years and the ships and their builders are worth detailing.

COASTAL PASSENGER SHIPS

The Newport News SB & DD Co was by far the biggest builder and in 1923 turned out the CITY OF CHATTANOOGA and CITY OF BIRMINGHAM for the Ocean SS Co of Savannah, steamship owners since 1877. Next year came the 5,100 grt turbine steamers GEORGE WASHINGTON and ROBERT E. LEE, ordered for the Old Dominion Line which was acquired by Eastern SS Lines in 1923, running from New York to Norfolk, Va. No less than six ships were built during 1925-1927 for the Clyde SS Co; the single screw ships CHEROKEE, SEMINOLE, MOHAWK and ALGONQUIN of 5,900 grt carrying 450 passengers in the New York-Charleston-Jacksonville service and IROQUOIS and SHAWNEE, twin screw, 6,500 grt, ships for the New York-Florida run.

The COAMO, 7,050 grt was also delivered in 1925 for the New York & Porto Rico SS Co and three ships in 1926 for the Merchants & Miners Tn Co., 5,600 grt, carrying 320 passengers for service from Boston, Philadelphia and Baltimore to Savannah and Jacksonville. They were named CHATHAM, DORCHESTER and FAIRFAX. Also in 1927 the twin screw turbine steamer CARACAS was built for the New York-West Indies service of the Atlantic & Caribbean SN Co.

Other ships in this five-year period came from the Federal SB & DD Co at Kearny, NJ, a subsidiary of the U.S. Steel Corp., these being the ALLEGHENY and BERKSHIRE, 5,500 grt with accommodation for 300 passengers. They were for the Merchants & Miners Tn Co. Federal also built a cargo ship in 1925 for the railway-owned Southern Pacific SS Lines. Turbine driven, she was the EL OCEANO, 6,770 grt but flew the Panamanian flag. At Sparrows Point, the Bethlehem Steel Co built the BOSTON and NEW YORK in 1924, two twin-screw ships for the Boston-New York service of Eastern SS Lines. One other notable ship turned out by this yard in the same year was the 2,367 grt ALEXANDER HAMILTON for the Hudson River Day Line. She was propelled by paddle wheels and was the last such steamer on the eastern seaboard of North America. She continued excursion runs, 150 miles up the Hudson River from New York to Albany until sold in 1962 to Circle Line Sightseeing Yachts Inc., eventually being withdrawn after making her last voyage on the Hudson River on 6 September 1971.

THE 1928 ACT

In May 1928, the Jones-White Act was passed which gave the Treasury powers to lend shipowners money up to 75% of building or alteration costs on very easy repayment terms, as well as mail subsidies to keep the ships operating. The underlying motive of the Act was to provide reserve auxiliaries for the US Navy. This Act prompted a quick response and a number of larger ships were laid down in the ensuing years, some of very much larger design for the inter-coastal trade which had progressed since the Panama Canal was opened in August 1914.

Again, it was the Newport News company which turned out the greatest number of ships. Three large liners were built for the Panama-Pacific branch of the International Mercantile Marine Co — CALIFORNIA and PENNSYLVANIA in 1928, VIRGINIA in 1929. Each was of 20,000 grt, two funnelled and propelled by turbo-electric machinery and twin screws. The CALIFORNIA measured 601 ft oa 574 ft bp x 80 ft, the others slightly larger at 613 ft oa, 588 ft bp. They were very successful on the New York-California route but were eventually overwhelmed by rail competition and in 1938 moved to Moore-McCormack & Co who rebuilt them with one funnel for the 'Good Neighbour' service, New York to South America. Under the guise of the American Republics Line, they became URUGUAY, ARGENTINA and BRAZIL.

In the following year came the MORRO CASTLE and ORIENTE for the New York-Havana service of the 1881-established Ward Line (New York & Cuba Mail SS Co). Also of turbo-electric drive they were 11,500 grt and could carry 430 passengers. The MORRO CASTLE was afire on 8 March 1934 off New Jersey and was a total loss.

Next came the larger Dollar liners, PRESIDENT HOOVER and PRESIDENT COOLIDGE, 22,000 grt, twin screw and again turbo-electric drive. They sailed from the West coast of the US to the Orient. The first named went aground on 11 December 1937 at Hoisho Island off Formosa on voyage San Francisco to Kobe and Manila and was sold for breaking up.

These were the largest ships of the period built at Newport News, the remainder, in the early 1930s being a coasting steamer, FLORIDA for the Peninsular & Occidental SS Co., two more for the Eastern SS Lines named SAINT JOHN and ACADIA and two for the Caribbean service of the Colombia Mail SS Co — COLOMBIA and HAITI. There were also three fruit ships constructed for the United Fruit Co — URIQUI, PETEN and TALAMANCA as well as the previously mentioned cargo steamers for A.H. Bull & Co., ANGELINA and MANUELA.

Turning to Bethlehem Steel Co shipbuilding, apart from the Sparrows Point yard, the Quincy yard at Boston, Mass., built a number of interesting ships commencing in 1929 with two 4,400 grt (6,600 tdw) colliers BERWINDGLEN and BERWINDVALE. They were for the Wilmore SS Co Inc., a subsidiary of the Berwind-White Coal Mining Co Inc., and were used in the coastal trade, Hampton Roads-Boston-Bath (Maine) range. One was driven by triple expansion engines, the other by steam turbine. They also built the 7,100 grt BORINQUEN for the New York & Porto Rico SS Co in 1931.

In the 1931-1932 period three large passenger liners were delivered to the Matson Navigation Co for service from San Francisco, Los Angeles — Honolulu and Australia. They were the LURLINE, MONTEREY and MARIPOSA, twin screw, two funnelled ships carrying 700 passengers in two classes. The LURLINE has sailed for Chandris Lines under the Greek flag as the ELLINIS since 1963 and the MONTEREY (renamed MATSONIA in 1956 and LURLINE in 1963) since 1970 as the BRITANIS. The MARIPOSA became Home Line's HOMERIC in 1953. Other ships of 1932 were three fruit ships for United Mail SS Co (United Fruit Co), ANTIGUA, QUIRIGUA and VERAGUA, part of an order for six of which three came from Newport News.

In 1927 the Federal SB & DD Co built the DIXIE, an 8,200 grt coastal passenger ship for the Southern Pacific SS Lines and then were given orders for four inter-coastal ships for the Grace Line. Twin screw, turbine ships they competed with the Panama-Pacific Line's 'big three', sailing from New York via many Caribbean and Mexican ports to Los Angeles and San Francisco. But with the grinding depression of the early 1930s the company finally closed the service in 1937. The ships, SANTA(s) ROSA, LUCIA, PAULA and ELENA were switched to other services.

At the New York SB Corp., yard at Camden there was a resurgence of building when the SANTA CLARA was built in 1930. Also for the Grace Line, she was just over 8,000 grt, twin screw and steam turbine. She was for the New York-Panama-West South America coast run. Four more ships in 1930-1931 formed the 'Four Aces' round-the-world service of the American Export Lines. They were 9,300 grt turbine ships named EXCALIBUR, EXOCHORDA, EXETER and EXCAMBION. The New York SB Corp., formed in 1899, built all types of ships.

In the immediate pre-war years and thereafter the yard was used essentially to construct naval ships. Two notable merchant ship buildings of 1932-1933 were the large North Atlantic passenger liners MANHATTAN and WASHINGTON for the United States Lines. These ships were given six steam turbines geared to twin screws. Both became troopships in 1941, but apart from two tankers for the Socony-Vacuum Oil Co Inc., in 1935, no other merchant ships were constructed by the New York SB Corp Inc., until 1950.

Apart from the Great Lakes yards of the American SB Co., Lorain; Great Lakes Engineering Works, River Rouge; the Manitowoc SB Corp., and Toledo SB Co which turned out a number of bulk carriers for Great Lakes service, only three other yards in the United States were in the building lists. These were the Sun SB Co at Chester Pa., mostly concerned with tanker construction but which built the passenger/cargo liner CITY OF NEW YORK for the American South African Line in 1930 and the 'Seatrain' ships and the old pioneer Delaware River shipbuilding yard of Wm Cramp & Sons which turned out the coastal passenger ships YARMOUTH and EVANGELINE for the Boston-New York-Canadian province ports service of Eastern SS Lines in 1927 as well as the 17,300 grt MALOLO for the Matson Company. One other yard to be mentioned is the Todd Drydock & Construction Co., at Tacoma, Wash., which built the 8,000 grt coastal passenger steamer BIENVILLE in 1924. This was the last large steamer to be built on the West coast until 1939.

This then was the picture of the US merchant ship fleet of the early 1930s — a fairly modern domestic coastwise passenger fleet, a generally up-to-date tanker fleet with many ships engaged in the Gulf-East coast domestic trade and a large number of slow and ageing dry cargo steamers.

DRIFT TO WAR

At this time the world was becoming uneasy through the rapidly deteriorating international political situation. Already in the Far East, Japanese forces had occupied some Chinese mainland coastal areas, Germany was astir with re-armament on an increasing scale, Spaniard was facing Spaniard in a coming civil war whilst the Italian army began facing Abyssinian forces on the borders of Italian Somaliland. Already, in 1930, Japan had notified her intention to withdraw from the London Naval Limitation Agreement and it was not long before other naval powers began their vast expansion programmes, substantial US Navy orders being placed in 1934.

The United States at this time possessed not only one of the largest navies in the world but a merchant marine of some 3,000 vessels, totalling 12 million gross tons, second only to the British Empire with relative figures of 9,000 and 20 million. But, as already stated, apart from the Great Lakes bulk carriers, there had been no dry cargo ship construction since the immediate postwar years. A considerable number of the war-built ships were in reserve and the average remaining life of the merchant fleet was five years. The US Government was fully aware of the facts and with the worrying international situation was also mindful of the need for fast merchant ships that could quickly be adapted to the role of naval auxiliaries, should the need arise.

THE MERCHANT MARINE ACT OF 1936

In 1936 came the Merchant Marine Act which again, as with other previous Acts, embodied the same common features — the support of the Merchant Marine and of the Navy through auxiliaries, the continual striving for more and more efficiency in the ships, in their safety and their crews and the formation of an organisation to administer these policies.

Under the mandate of the Act the United States Maritime Commission was formed on 26 October 1936, charged with responsibility to develop and build up the US Merchant Marine and fulfil the premises of the Act.

The Act called for the abolition of the old hidden subsidy of ocean-mail contracts in which some abuse had occurred. By the middle of 1937 claims by twenty-three operating companies for thirty-two mail contracts had been settled and the few remaining were settled in the following months.

All these were replaced with operating-differential subsidy agreements, these being a new concept in government aid. United States operators, faced with foreign competition on important trade routes, could transport cargo at the foreign rates, the difference between these and the rates of US ship operation which included wages, insurance, repairs and maintenance being recouped from the Treasury.

Another important premise of the Act was the reduction of government participation in ship operation and by March 1940 all government operation of lines had been run down and transferred to private companies on competitive bids.

There was also a differential subsidy arrangement enabling shipping companies to bring their costs in line with foreign competitors in the building of ships so that capital costs would be no higher than those in European yards where both construction and labour costs were cheaper.

The shipping position at the time of the establishment of the Maritime Commission necessitated some immediate contracts to be awarded. After heavy financial losses on the North Atlantic in the summer of 1934, the LEVIATHAN had been withdrawn with government permission under the condition that another vessel be built to run with the WASHINGTON and MANHATTAN. Agreement was reached and the LEVIATHAN was laid up in September 1934, eventually sailing from New York in January 1938 and arriving at the breakers at Rosyth on 14 February 1938. Plans were prepared for the new ship and the contract to build was awarded just previous to the final voyage of the LEVIATHAN, in October 1937. This vessel, appropriately, was to be the symbol of the revitalised United States Merchant Marine — ss AMERICA — Hull No 1 of the Maritime Commission's new programme.

The second urgent order was for a group of fast tankers. They were of joint US Navy/Maritime Commission design, fast, turbine driven, twin screw ships. They included defence features in their build paid for by the US Navy and were for naval use if necessity demanded. Twelve were ordered and were given MC Hull Nos 2-13.

Thirdly, the Commission, looking towards the training of seamen, took over a ship that had been laid up for some time. This was the EDGEMOOR, a steam turbine vessel completed by the Skinner & Eddy Corp., as Yard No. 48 at Seattle in May 1919 for the US Shipping Board. Taken over in 1938, she was allocated to the Coast Guard to operate. In May 1939 she completed conversion to a training ship at Bethlehem Steel Co., Baltimore Md. She was renamed AMERICAN SEAMAN. With measurements of 410 ft bp in length x 54 ft breadth giving 7,111 grt, she could accommodate 300 apprentice seamen. She was based later at the training school at St Petersburg, Florida and was eventually broken up by the Patapsco Co., Baltimore, in 1952.

MARITIME COMMISSION TRAINING SHIPS

Several other ships were requisitioned by the Maritime Commission for use as training ships in the early stages of the war:
AMERICAN SAILOR 7,129 grt ex EDGEMONT-1941. Built by Skinner & Eddy Corp., Seattle (Yard No 46) and converted by Bethlehem Steel Co., Baltimore in July 1941;
two coastal passenger ships from the Merchant & Miners Tn Co:
AMERICAN ENGINEER 5,861 grt ex BERKSHIRE-1941. Built by the Federal SB & DD Co, Kearny (Yard No 73) 1923.
AMERICAN SEAFARER 5,456 grt ex ALLEGHENY-1941. Built by the Federal SB & DD Co Kearny (Yard No 73) 1923.
another coastal passenger ship from the Ocean SS Co of Savannah:
AMERICAN NAVIGATOR 5,861 grt ex CITY OF CHATTANOOGA-1941. Built by the Newport News SB & DD Co (Yard No 266) 1923;
an ex-naval vessel:
AMERICAN PILOT 5,524 grt ex USS EMPIRE STATE (IX 38)-1940, ex USS PROCYON (AG 11)-1921, ex SHAUME. Built by the American International SB Co., Hog Island (Yard No 528) 1919;
and an early-built, Liberty-type steamer converted before completion:
AMERICAN MARINER 7,100 grt launched as GEORGE CALVERT. Built by the Bethlehem-Fairfield Yard, Baltimore and converted 1943.
There were also a number of yachts and sailing vessels acquired.

GENERAL DESIGNS OF STANDARD SHIPS

Meanwhile the Maritime Commission was planning the new merchant marine. There were two ways of choosing the ships to be built. The first was to carefully examine each trade route and then consult the operators of that route to obtain their views of the particular characteristics needed in the ships for that route. This process however, was considered to be too lengthy and the second way was chosen. This was to outline the characteristics of several types of ships covering the deadweight capacity and a balance of speed and then prepare suitable designs and specifications of the types. It was realised that a chosen design might not be entirely adequate for the route to be served but provision for minor changes would be made to meet particular requirements of the route. The basic plans and specifications fell into these groups.

The original design, that of a non-passenger carrying type and known as C2, was selected because the Commission believed this size, capacity and speed to be the most urgent replacement needed by the US Merchant Marine. The specifications and plans were drawn up and forwarded to a number of marine architects, shipbuilders and shipowners for comment and a number of suggestions were received, one of which was to alter the design from six to five cargo holds and this suggestion was adopted.

The next type was that of a 10,000 tons cargo capacity vessel, although a passenger/cargo vessel was at first envisaged. The plans for the ship — C3 type — were circularised, but in this instance, so many contradictory and impracticable suggestions were forthcoming that only a few were adopted.

However, the ship was quite satisfactory to operators. Some later variations included plans for the carrying of 97, 111, 155 and 192 passengers in four groups of ships.

The third type was the smaller C1 ship and in this respect the Commission chose a different policy. When plans and specifications were drawn up they were circularised to the operators who had shown interest in a smaller capacity ship during the early stages of its development and from comments received it was clear that two classes of the C1 type would be required — a shelter deck class to obtain a large cubic capacity and a full scantling class of ship for greater deadweight capacity.

Propelling machinery of the new ships was either steam or diesel — steam turbine driving a single screw through double reduction gearing; a single diesel engine to a single screw direct; two-set engines driving single screws through gearing and four-set engines also operating a single screw through gearing.

This then was the basis of the new fleet. Efficient carriers as any on the high seas and each one readily convertible for naval use.

Private demand from the shipping companies for the building of the ships was however, not forthcoming in sufficient volume to ensure the replacement of the ageing merchant ships of World War I vintage and the Commission promulgated a modest plan, approved by the Executive, for the building of fifty ships per year for the ensuing ten years which would place 500 ships of nearly 4 million gross tons of shipping under the US flag; some to be privately owned, some to be owned by the Commission and chartered out to operators.

FIRST CONTRACTS

In late 1937-1938, in the tense state of the international situation, contracts were let for the first fifty ships — the liner AMERICA in October 1937, the twelve national defence tankers for private operation but with defence features paid for by the US Navy, on 5 January 1938, twenty C2 type ships, fourteen C3 type ships (of which four were to American Export Line's private design in co-operation with the Commission) and three combination passenger/cargo ships for the Mississippi Shipping Co's Delta Line.

By the end of August 1939, twenty-four ships were ordered and these included ten C3 passenger/cargo ships, six C3 cargo ships, three C2 and the first orders for five C1 type vessels.

At Newport News on 31 August 1939 a crowd of 30,000 assembled to witness the launch of the ss AMERICA, the greatest and most luxurious liner ever built in the United States but the general topic at the luncheon which followed was the serious international situation. Indeed, the launching story was almost blanketed in the press for next day the storm broke — Germany invaded Poland and two days after that Europe was at war.

The Commission immediately speeded up its programme, for not only were merchant ships required, but the US Navy was now acquiring the C-type hulls for conversion to fleet auxiliaries. A further seventy-one ships were ordered in the last four months of 1939 and the position on the last day of the year was that of 145 ships of 1,145,517 grt ordered, twenty-one of 176,367 grt were in service.

These large orders almost completely dominated the shipbuilding yards which took some time to assimilate the work and only seven private orders were made in 1939. The following year thirty-six Maritime Commission orders were given with thirteen other ships to private contract.

OPERATING SUBSIDIES

Under the operating provisions of the Merchant Marine Act of 1936, shipping operators had to build new vessels in order to qualify for payments which covered the difference in cost of operating a vessel under American legislation with higher wages, a reduced number of working hours and better working conditions than other foreign-flag ships.

Following the inception of the Act the undermentioned shipping companies in the United States received operating differential subsidy although subsidised operations were not made between 31 March 1942 and 31 December 1946.

During the lifetime of the Maritime Commission fifteen companies signed agreements to run from 1 July 1937:

American Diamond Lines Inc (ended 1938)
American Export Lines Inc
American Mail Line Inc
American South African Line Inc (from March 1948 Farrell Lines)
Atlantic & Caribbean SN Co
Baltimore Mail SS Co (ended 1938)
Grace Line Inc
Lykes Bros SS Co Inc
Mississippi Shipping Co (from April 1962 Delta SS Lines)
Moore-McCormack Lines Inc
New York & Cuba Mail SS Co
Oceanic SS Co
Pacific Argentine Brazil Line Inc (ended 1939 but again 1949-1956)
South Atlantic SS Co (ended 1938)
United States Lines
and a further two in 1938:
25 January 1938 Dollar SS Lines (from 1 November 1938 American President Lines)
14 October 1938 Seas Shipping Co (ended August 1957)

ACCELERATION OF SHIPBUILDING

Britain, at this time standing alone and facing the jubilant might of German armies along the seaboard of western Europe and also facing serious shipping losses, ordered sixty standard ships from the United States in December 1940. These were the 'Ocean'-type. On 22 June 1941 Germany invaded the USSR in the escalating war and in July the US Expansion Act increased the authorised tonnage of the US Navy by 70% — a two-ocean Navy being deemed very necessary. With this decision came the need for auxiliary ships from merchant hulls.

Then, on 7 December 1941 came the holocaust of Pearl Harbor. Ships were now not only requested for Naval use but for Army use as well and with sinkings running into $\frac{1}{2}$ million gross tons per month the need for ships on the North Atlantic was intense.

More building ways were added to existing yards; more new yards were built, wave following wave of shipbuilding expansion coming as the United States went to war in the knowledge that no maritime nation had ever successfully emerged from conflict without naval auxiliary and merchant fleet support.

So it went on, ships of all types being turned out in record times, these times being beaten in turn by fresh records. Transports, tugs, landing craft, cargo ships and even naval frigates were built under Maritime Commission jurisdiction. All told, from 1939 until 1945, 5,171 ships of over 2,000 grt were built under Maritime Commission control, totalling 38,500,000 grt of shipping with a carrying capacity of 54,700,000 tons.

WAR SHIPPING ADMINISTRATION

For the most effective operation of the ever-growing fleet of merchant ships for wartime, an organisation known as the War Shipping Administration was established in February 1942. Its job was to collaborate with Army, Navy and Civil departments and other Government agencies to obtain the best use of shipping and take over the control of the country's merchant ships.

The ships outside the arrangement were the combatant vessels of the Army, the Navy and Coast Guard and the ships under the control of the Office of Defense Transportation, ie those engaged in coastwise, intercoastal and inland transport.

Some 75% of the country's cargo ships, passenger liners and tankers had been requisitioned by mid-April 1942 and all remaining ships were subject of a requisition order made on 18 April 1942.

This arrangement ceased in September 1946.

AUXILIARY SHIPS

There are so many functions a navy has to perform that apart from the combatant ships of the fleet there is need for numerous types of supporting vessels.

An early type of auxiliary was the collier when ships were far from home and naval strategy called for coaling stations in many remote islands and territories the world over. Thus the collier became the feeder ship to those stations without which, of course, the far-based ships could not operate. When the navies turned to oil-burning machinery for their ships the collier was gradually ousted and a new type of auxiliary was introduced — the fleet oiler.

Then there are the tenders which victual, re-store and refuel the destroyers, submarines, motor torpedo boats; carrying out all manner of repairs and at the same time acting as a kind of rest club for officers and men of the group of ships served. Hospital ships, salvage ships, naval cargo ships, transports, tugs — all these also come under the category of auxiliary.

With the expansion of the US Navy in pre-war years, merchant ship hulls began to be acquired from the Maritime Commission to become auxiliaries. Many were taken over before completion as merchant ships for conversion to differing types.

Between 1939 and 1945 about 1,000 ships were delivered by the Maritime Commission to the US Navy. About half this number consisted of combat ships, the Attack Transports, Attack Cargo ships, Escort Carrier conversions and Frigates. Some 300 vessels were purely cargo carriers and included many C, Liberty and Victory type ships and about half that number again consisted of the smaller craft — the coasters, tugs and barges.

The Attack Transports, Attack Cargo ships and the larger Landing Ships formed the core of the amphibious forces and operated close inshore, the Attack ships disgorging troops in self-borne Landing Craft and assisting in the assault-covering fire power.

Of the Attack ships there were 229 transports (APA) of which 211 were from Maritime Commission contracts. Of these there were 57 x C3 hulls, 7 x C2 hulls and 113 Victory hulls as well as 32 specially designed ships of the S4-SE2-BD1 type and the P1-S2-L2 19-knot ships DOYEN and FELAND. Among the other eighteen pre-war ships were the 'Four Aces' of the American Export Lines, well known on the Mediterranean service and the five ships of the Baltimore Mail SS Co. All the Attack Cargo ships (AKA) were Maritime Commission vessels and comprised 74 x C2 hulls and 32 specially designed S4-SE2-BE1 type ships. The total of 108 was made up by one C3-E type vessel and one C1 ship, later designated AK. The escort carrier conversions and frigates are the subjects of special sections.

As the US forces gradually swept westwards across the Pacific Ocean, islands were re-occupied to form advanced bases and these became worked and fed by the repair ships, stores ships, tankers, salvage ships and netlayers; cargo ships, ammunition ships and small petrol carriers — auxiliaries to tend and support the advancing forces.

Converted Maritime Commission ships also served as tenders. In 1939 there were eight destroyer tenders (AD), increasing to eleven by 1943, all US Navy-built. Also acquired for conversion during the 1940-1944 period were fourteen C3 hulls, although four of these were cancelled when war ended.

From a nucleus of five submarine tenders (AS) in 1939, seven 'Fulton'-class ships were added by the Navy whilst another seven C3 and one C1 hulls were converted. Among the many ships converted to Motor torpedo boat tenders (AGP) were two C1 hulls and many Tank Landing ships whilst seven C3 hulls were modified for use as Seaplane Tenders (AV).

Supply ships were particularly numerous. There were two old Ammunition ships (AE) in 1939 but this number was quickly increased by several C2 hulls of which twelve were converted and another three modified and built by the Navy. There was also one C1 type ship. Most were named after volcanoes.

Stores ships (AF) for carrying meat and other perishable foods necessitated extensive refrigerated space and apart from ten ships of the United Fruit Co which were taken over, there were four C2 hulls and seventeen of the R1-M-AV3 types.

Some 200 ships were acquired as Cargo carriers (AK) for the Navy from the original five at the commencement of war and these included Liberty, Victory and C-type ships. The latter included 65 of the C1-M-AV1 design and there were 66 Liberty and ten Victory ships. Some Liberty ships were re-designated.

Hospital ships (AH) were operated by both Navy and Army. The five early Navy ships were soon supplemented by three C1-B vessels converted before completion and later on, six of the larger C4-type ships were taken over.

Numerous transports (AP) included a host of pre-war requisitioned liners. Later came the P2 ships and thirty C4 vessels commissioned as transports and a number of C2 vessels. The AP designations reached 177 ships but 58 of these were re-designated AKA in 1942. Three became hospital ships and a number went to the Army.

These were the bulk of the auxiliary ship types which had Maritime Commission hulls although there were other smaller classes — Repair Ships (AR), Distilling Ships (AW), Fleet Tugs (AT), Rescue ships (ATR) etc.

TROOP TRANSPORTS

As stated, there were numerous troop transports, for the military forces of the United States were fighting on foreign soil many thousands of miles from their homeland.

Not only did the US Navy run troopships but so did the Army and the War Shipping Administration.

The Army had owned troopships for a long time and these were controlled by the Quartermaster General. This was altered so that the control came under the Transportation Corps.

Although a number of ships were owned by the Army, many more were bareboat chartered. Some however, were taken on loan without time charter hire from the War Shipping Administration. Sixty-five major ships were operated by the Army as troop transports during the war and these were usually civilian crewed with Army personnel in administrative capacity.

One of the largest transports operated by the Army was the GEORGE WASHINGTON (23,788 grt), built at Stettin in 1909 for the Norddeutscher Lloyd's North Atlantic service. Interned at New York in 1917 she was ceded to the US Government and in 1931 became a transport. In 1941 she was temporarily named CATLIN. There was also the 21,339 grt EDMUND B ALEXANDER built at Belfast in 1905 as the Hamburg Amerika Line's AMERIKA. She too, was ceded to the US in 1921 and changed her name to AMERICA. Both these ships also sailed under Navy control for a period.

Two ships from the New York & Cuba Mail SS Co — CHARLES A. STAFFORD, originally the SIBONEY of 1918 vintage and a one-time hospital ship and the 1930-built ORIENTE, renamed THOMAS H. BARRY also sailed as Army troopships. Other old tonnage included the 1920-built ST MIHIEL and CHATEAU THIERRY, both hospital ships which also sailed under US Navy control for some time and U.S. GRANT, built as KONIG WILHELM II in Germany in 1907.

Naval transports (designated AP) carried Army personnel and there was also a large group of attack transports (APA). The ships were under the direction of the Naval Transportation Service — an organisation which came into being in January 1942.

In 1939 the US Navy possessed only two transports, HENDERSON 7,500 grt, 1916 (AP1) and CHAUMONT 7,500 grt, 1921 (AP5). These were supplemented in 1939-1940 by the WILLIAM WARD BURROWS (AP6) a Grace liner of 4,600 grt built in 1929 and the much larger WHARTON (AP7) of 13,800 grt. This was the old Munson SS Co's SOUTHERN CROSS, built in 1920. In 1940-1941 many more were acquired including two American President liners, two Grace liners and all five ships of the Baltimore Mail Line. All three liners of the United States Line's North Atlantic service were also acquired in 1941, the MANHATTAN, WASHINGTON and AMERICA being renamed WAKEFIELD (AP21), MOUNT VERNON (AP22) and WEST POINT (AP23) respectively. By the end of 1941 thirty six vessels were sailing or converting as troop transports for the US Navy.

Troopships were operated by the War Shipping Administration from the date of its creation in February 1942 to enable more efficient allocation of vessels, for even before December 1941 ships were interchanged between Army and Navy as requirements dictated, on bareboat charter, space charter, loan basis etc in rather cumbersome fashion.

Many of the new C-type vessels were also allocated to the three operating agencies — Army, Navy and WSA for conversion to troop carriers. Some of these were of the combination passenger/cargo type but although passenger accommodation was already fitted, to carry troops in large numbers, cargo space had to be taken over for additional berths and messes, toilets and medical facilities. If the ships were simply of the cargo type then apart from the above, living quarters for medical, military and signal detachments had to be provided and offices, baggage space and strong rooms made. All troop compartments had to be heated, ventilated and provided with two exit stairways and generally, no troops were berthed below the waterline. A further rule was that patients in hospital on ships were to be carried not more than two decks below the lifeboat deck.

The ships had armament manned at first by the Army, but later by naval gunners. The hulls were camouflaged and fitted with degaussing coils and for travelling in convoys, signalling equipment — lights, flags, range finders etc and black-out screens were fitted. Some ships, hurriedly taken up for conversion in the immediate pre-war period, were later more permanently converted.

CLASSIFICATION OF AUXILIARIES

The auxiliary ships were numbered and prefixed with the letter A — AK, AD etc, this designation dating back to 1921. The US Navy at that time was coal-driven so the letter C was allocated to colliers, T was given to tugs, D to destroyers, N to netlayers, H to Hospital ships and R to repair ships. However, with the letter T already used, the transport was allocated P and cargo ship K.

In those days the auxiliaries were non-combatant and carried the prefix A, thus AK was a naval auxiliary and a cargo ship. When the United States entered the war in 1941 the auxiliary became more intimately involved with the enemy but although some ships became attack ships with APA and AKA designations, the prefix A still classified the ship as an auxiliary although some personnel could probably remember the earlier designation of APA as Animal Transport. For a list of designations relative to this book see page 10.

POST WAR DISPOSALS

As the war neared its end the problems arose of the future of the huge fleet of merchant ships then under the United States flag. In some circles it was considered that with the total absence of German and Japanese ships there would be enough foreign trade to keep the ships under the US flag, but this certainly would have upset the allies who had lost much of their merchant tonnage and who, far more than the US, were dependent on merchant ships for the earning of foreign currency, particularly dollars with which to purchase US exports. Indeed, the US fleet in peacetime had, from experience, found less profits for its operators than other sectors of the economy and it was probable that the maintenance of the huge fleet would have had to be subsidized with money from the exchequer to keep it in operation.

In the end it was deemed right that the international shipping market should be restored to a competitive basis, with the opportunity for United States owners and foreign owners to purchase ships.

About 1,000 ships were required to maintain the domestic and some foreign trade of the United States and a reserve of ships was also provided so that in the event of hostilities the country would not have to devote a major part of its war effort to a crash shipbuilding programme. The remaining ships were offered for sale or were distributed to allies at very attractive terms so that even the slow Liberty ship would be an attractive acquisition.

In February 1946 the United States Congress passed the Merchant Ship Sales Act of 1946 and there then began the disposal of the tremendous fleet.

The Act defined a war-built ship as an ocean-going vessel of 1,500 or more tons, owned by the United States, suitable for commercial use, which was constructed or contracted for by or for the account of the United States between 1 January 1942 and 2 September 1945 or, having been constructed during the period 3 September 1939 to 2 September 1945, was acquired by the United States during that period.

The statutory sales price for a dry-cargo vessel was fixed at 50% of the pre-war domestic cost of that type and a tanker at 87½% of the pre-war domestic cost. The domestic cost was the amount determined by the Maritime Commission for which a standard ship could have been built in the U.S. in normal conditions in (about) January 1942. The higher rate for tankers was fixed as it was considered they would be used in the domestic trade of the U.S. and would therefore be shielded from foreign competition by the US cabotage laws. All ships sold would have a price adjustment of 5% per annum for depreciation from the delivery date and a further adjustment for any deterioration due to war service.

The floor price for dry cargo ships was fixed at 35% of the domestic war cost (ie: average construction cost without any national defence features) with tankers at 50%. Liberty ships were at 31½%.

No foreign sales were permitted of passenger-type, bulk dry cargo or tankers of the Liberty type but ten C-type which were already under foreign charter were permitted immediate sale.

The bill also provided for the acquisition by the Maritime Commission of ships in exchange for an allowance on credit on the purchase of war-built ships.

The closing date for placing in reserve of vessels unsold within the time limit was 31 December 1947 but this was later extended for United States citizens to 1950.

The bill was quite successful in providing the US government the means of withdrawing from the shipping business and at the same time helping to restore the balance of international shipping.

THE US MERCHANT FLEET RESERVE

As decreed in the Merchant Ship Sales Act of 1946, those ships remaining unsold at the end of 1950 were placed in the National Defence Reserve fleets in 1951.

By far the greatest number of ships were of the Liberty-type but there were some 300 Victory ships and about 100 C-type ships of the larger variation. There were also about 100 dry cargo coastal ships but only a very few tankers.

These ships were placed in eight fleets and the lay-up sites were at:

Hudson River, near Nyack, New York
James River off Lee Hall, near Newport News, Virginia
Wilmington, North Carolina
Mobile, Alabama
Beaumont, Texas
Suisun Bay, Martinez, near San Francisco, California
Columbia River, Astoria, Oregon
Puget Sound, Olympia, Washington

As circumstances dictated, they were withdrawn from lay-up for the emergencies of the Korean war, the Suez crisis of 1956 and Viet-Nam and were also used for the Ship Exchange Act which permitted non-subsidised obsolete US-flag tonnage to be traded in on a price differential basis for better class war-built ships from the Reserve fleets, although those traded in were mostly soon sold for scrapping.

The ships were placed under the care of the Maritime Commission, although on 25 May 1950 the US Department of Commerce (Federal Maritime Board) assumed the functions of the US Maritime Commission and the controlling body became known as the Maritime Administration (MARAD).

Gradually, as the fleets dwindled, sites were abandoned, the first being that at Wilmington and then the one at Astoria. By mid-1970 six sites remained, although greatly depleted with the continuing sale of obsolete ships. During 1971 the Hudson River site was closed down and the following year saw the closure of the one at Olympia, Washington. The site at Mobile, Alabama, was scheduled for closure during 1974 whilst the three remaining sites retain the vessels considered suitable for possible reactivation.

The liner AMERICA leaving Newport News for trials in 1940 *U.S.M.C.*

The liner AMERICA as the troopship WEST POINT *U.S.N.*

The liner AMERICA in post-war colours *Skyfotos*

PART ONE

ss **AMERICA** — the symbol

P4-S2 type

In October 1937 the awarding of the contract to build the liner AMERICA signified the start of the '500 ships within 10 years' programme of the United States Maritime Commission — a programme which was designed to return the United States to a more dominant position on the oceans of the world.

She was, at that time, the largest passenger liner to be constructed in the United States and was hailed as a symbol of the new US Merchant Marine. Hull No 1 of the Maritime Commission programme, she was Yard No 369 of her builders, the Newport News SB & DD Co., who laid her keel on 22 August 1938.

Fitted with the most modern safety devices, her decking was laid over steel, stateroom bulkheads were of asbestos compound, furniture of steel or aluminium and upholstery fireproof. Watertight subdivision was such that should three adjacent watertight compartments become flooded, the vessel would not submerge beyond a line three inches below and parallel to the highest continuous watertight deck. Fourteen lifeboats and two rescue boats were fitted.

Originally designed to carry 543 Cabin class, 418 Tourist and 241 Third class passengers and a crew of 643, it was the intention that she would sail in the United States Lines' North Atlantic service taking the place of the LEVIATHAN (59,956 grt, 1914) which had been withdrawn from service in 1935. From New York to Hamburg, the wayports were to be Cobh, Plymouth, Southampton and Havre and for running partners she was to have the MANHATTAN (24,289 grt, 1932) and the WASHINGTON (24,289 grt, 1933).

On 31 August 1939 she was christened AMERICA by Mrs Franklin D. Roosevelt in the presence of some 30,000 people, the day prior to the outbreak of war in Europe and by the time she was completed in June 1940 the Neutrality Act had caused the North Atlantic service of United States Lines to cease.

For a time she cruised to the West Indies, commencing on 10 August 1940 until the Spring of 1941 when she was altered to carry 8,175 troops. She commenced trooping in the June under her new name of WEST POINT (AP 23) and in the following year, on 28 September 1942, was acquired by the US Navy.

On 22 February 1946 she finished her war service and on 28 February was transferred from the US Navy to the War Shipping Administration and given an eight-months reconditioning by her builders, making her maiden voyage in the North Atlantic service under her original name of AMERICA on 14 November 1946 from New York to Cobh, Southampton and Le Havre. She now carried 1,050 passengers in First, Cabin and Tourist accommodation, the term Third class having been abandoned.

She was quite distinctive in outward appearance with a slightly curved, raking stem and high freeboard forward. There were two widely spaced funnels, one very much forward. After a short while they were heightened and fitted with smoke deflector fins. Another distinctive feature was a glassed-in promenade deck, 514 ft in length, with windows extending from floor to ceiling. A total of twenty-three public rooms and a swimming pool were installed.

The propelling machinery, with a weight of 2,514 tons, consisted of two sets of steam turbines producing 34,000 shp, driving twin screws at 128 rpm and giving a service speed of 20 knots. On trials she reached 24·68 knots.

She continued on the North Atlantic for many years and then, in August 1964, approval was given for the sale of the AMERICA to A.J. & D.J. Chandris of Greece for their Europe-Australia service, the sale being conditional that she would not trade to U.S. ports for a period of five years.

The ship left Hampton Roads on 18 November 1964, arriving at Piraeus on 30 November and there she was altered to carry 2,000 passengers in one class. During this £2 million refit she was completely air-conditioned and an open-air swimming pool was added to her amenities.

Her new owners placed her under their one-ship concern Okeania S.A., a company registered in Liberia although she was to sail under the Panamanian flag. Renamed AUSTRALIS she left Piraeus on her first commercial voyage to Australia under Chandris colours on 21 August 1965 and thereafter used Southampton as her European terminal. Later she became registered under the Greek flag.

The AMERICA, in Chandris Line colours as AUSTRALIS *Author's collection*

In August 1977 it was announced that the ship was to make one further — single — voyage to Sydney/Auckland and would then be withdrawn from service and placed on the sale list. This voyage commenced from Southampton on 18 November 1977, just thirteen years to the day from when she first sailed under the Chandris houseflag.

Following a short period of lay-up at Timaru, New Zealand, she was sold early in 1978 to Panama-flag operators named Venture Cruise Lines, for some 5 million dollars. Returning to New York on 18 May she was renamed with her former name. AMERICA, and repainted to a blue hull and white upperworks. Her funnels were also blue, with a red band and black top.

On 30 June she commenced a series of cruises from New York, but was arrested by order of the U.S. District Court on her return from the first one. Sold at public auction, she returned to the Chandris fleet for just over 1 million dollars — just five months after the Greek company sold her for five times this amount. Still named AMERICA, the ship sailed from New York on 6 September, arriving at Piraeus on 20 September 1978. Refurbished and renamed ITALIS, her 1979 cruising season will commence in the Mediterranean.

Details:

Length	723 ft oa	Tonnages:	26,454 grt (US measurement).
	660 ft 7 in bp		33,532 grt (British measurement).
Beam moulded	93 ft 3 in		35,440 displacement, full load.
Loaded draught	32 ft 6 in		14,331 tdw, full load.
Depth moulded	45 ft 4 in		

Holds: 6

Cruising radius: 11,000 miles.

The C1 type

The C1-type vessels were the smallest of the three original types designed by the United States Maritime Commission. They were intended to be efficient and economical on routes that did not call for fast ships. The original design included accommodation for eight passengers.

There were originally four types of C1 ships. The C1-A version was a shelter deck type and both steam ships and motor vessels were constructed. Likewise, both steam and motor propelled ships of the C1-B type were built, these being of a full scantling design.

The general characteristics of all ships were the same. They had a raked stem and cruiser stern, superstructure amidships, two masts (one between holds 1-2 and one between holds 4-5) and a kingpost between holds 2-3. There were eight compartments in the hull, comprising forepeak, three holds forward, machinery space, two holds aft and the after peak. The compartments were separated by seven watertight bulkheads. Two complete decks extended fore and aft and a third deck was fitted forward of the machinery space.

However, there were differences, the full scantling (B) type of ship being, in fact, more strongly built than the shelter decker and for 200 tons additional weight in the hull there was an extra 1,500 tons deadweight capacity in both turbine and diesel B-type vessels. The bulkheads between the cargo holds on the A-type extended only to the second deck whilst in the B-type they were watertight to the weather deck. Thus, the deck which topped the watertight bulkheads was the freeboard deck for classification and load line purposes and the B-type ship could be loaded deeper and carry more cargo.

The measurements of the hatches were:

	Shelter deck A-type	Full scantling B-type
Hatch No 1	24 ft x 24 ft 9 in	24 ft x 27 ft
Hatch No 2	24 ft x 33 ft 9 in	24 ft x 42 ft 9 in
Hatch No 3	24 ft x 31 ft 6 in	24 ft x 24 ft 9 in
Hatch No 4	24 ft x 18 ft	24 ft x 18 ft
Hatch No 5	24 ft x 36 ft	24 ft x 36 ft

No 2 hatch in the B-type was of great help in the handling of special cargoes. In both types the handling equipment comprised 1 x 50 ton, 1 x 25 ton, and 12 x 5 ton capacity derricks. The 5 ton derricks were shared equally between the masts and kingpost, the 50 ton derrick was at No 2 hold and the 25 ton derrick at No 5. There were twelve electric winches. However, as the building programme progressed and the designs later altered to the dictates of trade and war, there was considerable variation in the mast/kingpost/derrick arrangements.

The propelling machinery in the steamships consisted of a cross compound, double reduction geared turbine unit, supplied with steam from two water tube boilers. The motor ships had two engines of the two stroke single-acting type, the drive being taken through two magnetic couplings and a reduction gear to a single propeller shaft.

Crew were accommodated amidships, being 43 persons on the turbine ships and 41 on the motor ships.

Designed details:

	Shelter deck:		Full scantling:	
	Steamship	Motorship	Steamship	Motorship
Length, overall	412 ft 3 in	412 ft 3 in	417 ft 9 in	417 ft 9 in
Length, bp	390 ft	390 ft	395 ft	395 ft
Breadth moulded	60 ft	60 ft	60 ft	60 ft
Depth moulded	37 ft 6 in	37 ft 6 in	37 ft 6 in	37 ft 6 in
Draught loaded	23 ft 6 in	23 ft 6 in	27 ft 6 in	27 ft 6 in
Gross tonnage	5,028	5,028	6,750	6,750
Net tonnage	2,820	2,820	4,800	4,800
Deadweight tonnage	6,240	6,440	7,815	8,015
Service speed	14 knots	14 knots	14 knots	14 knots

ANALYSIS OF C1 TYPE SHIPS BUILT

Year	C1-A (S)	C1-A (M)	C1-B (S)	C1-B (M)	C1-S-AY1
1940	—	—	5	—	—
1941	—	1	18	10	—
1942	5	10	5	—	—
1943	6	18	39	—	7
1944	6	17	18	—	6
1945	2	—	—	—	—
(Totals 173)	19	46	85	10	13

NAVAL AUXILIARIES

Ships of the C1-type completed or diverted for military or naval service included a group of thirteen, modified and completed as military transports and reclassified the C1-S-AY1 type. They were all lend/leased to Great Britain and were renamed with an 'Empire' prefix. They served as landing ships (LSI (L)), in 1944 being transferred to the Royal Navy and given racehorse names. Five were later fitted out for Pacific operations. Two were wartime losses and the remainder were returned to the United States when war ended.

The C1-A motorships CAPE CARTHAGE and CAPE FAREWELL were acquired after launching and completed for the US Navy as the motor torpedo boat tenders ACONTIUS and CYRENE. Another, CAPE LOOKOUT, became an attack cargo ship, FOMALHAUT, later being reclassed as an ammunition ship for a time. Also taken over in November 1942 as an ammunition ship was another C1-A type, CAPE SABLE. She was renamed SANGAY.

Of the B-type ships, the FRED MORRIS (I) was taken over in March 1941 as a submarine tender and renamed OTUS, being converted at Manila at the end of the year. She later became a repair ship. The second FRED MORRIS and CAPE JOHNSON, both built in 1944 became transports, the FRED MORRIS being renamed ARLINGTON. The ALCOA PARTNER served the US Navy as the cargo ship AURIGA. Other B-type ships taken over while building became the US Navy hospital ships COMFORT, HOPE and MERCY.

POSTWAR DISPOSALS

At the end of the war the Ship Sales Act of 1946 came into effect and the United States commenced the sale of their wartime excess tonnage. Of the C1 ships, sixteen had been lost during the war, only one of these being a marine casualty. Between 1 July 1946 and 31 March 1950, twenty-three were sold to US flag operators and another 48 were sold to foreign owners.

These were:

Norway		27 ships
Denmark		7
China		4
Egypt		2
Netherlands		2
New Zealand		2
Philippines		2
Panama		1
United Kingdom		1
	Total:	48 ships

Of the twenty-three ships sold for the US flag, six went to the Mississippi Shipping Co. Inc., (Delta Line) for service from the Gulf ports to the East coast of South America and six joined the Lykes fleet. Three went to the Isbrandtsen Co., two to the Ocean SS Co of Savannah and two to the Munargo Line Co (a subsidiary of the United Fruit Co). The other four were shared one each to the South Porto Rico Sugar Co., the New York & Cuba Mail SS Co., the United Mail SS Co and the Warren Petroleum Co., this last one for conversion to a liquid gas carrier.

By far the largest number of C1 ships sold to foreign flag owners went to Norway, twenty-seven ships moving to numerous owners among whom were Westfal-Larsen & Co (five ships) and Leif Hoegh & Co., Rederiet Odfjell, Mowinckels Rederi and Oivind Lorentzen with two ships each. Each of the other fourteen went to separate owners.

Seven ships went to Denmark, four to A.P. Moller's 'Maersk' fleet and three to J. Lauritzen & Co. Four ships of the C1-S-AY1 modification were sold to Chinese interests and although new names were allocated, the sale fell through. Two other ships of this type did move to the Egyptian flag of the Societe Misr de Nav Maritime SAE and served for many years in the Middle East area. Two went to the Philippine flag of the De la Rama SS Co; two to Holland and one to Panama.

Of the three which went to the British register, two joined the fleet of the Union SS Company of New Zealand as WAIRIMU and WAIRATA and the third became LA ESTANCIA of Buries, Markes & Co.

EARLY ORDERS

C1-B type

Of the early orders, that is until the end of 1940, Lykes Bros., were the predominant receivers of C1 ships, the Alcoa SS Co., and the United States Lines being next in order with the New York & Cuba Mail SS Co., American Mail Line, Bull Line (A.H. Bull & Co) and Moore, McCormack & Co also taking early deliveries.

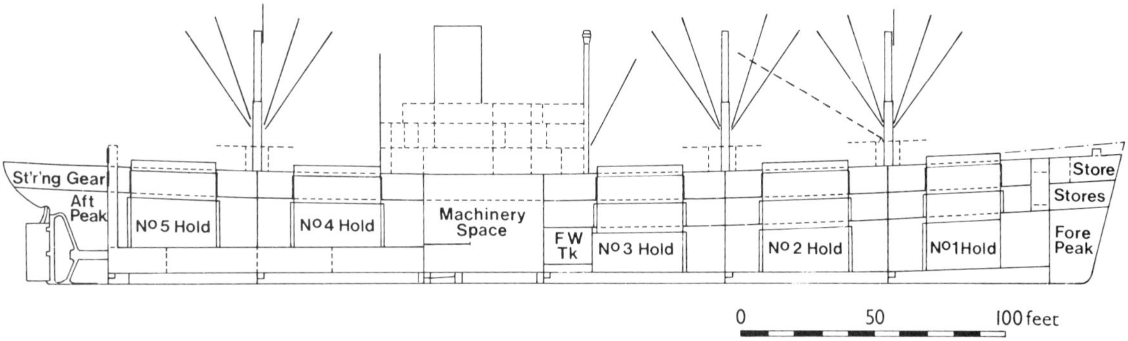

TYPICAL C1-B CARGO VESSEL

The first order for C1 ships was in August 1939 when five B-type, full scantling design turbine driven ships were ordered, all for Lykes Bros SS Co., to be delivered in the winter of 1940-41. With these vessels the masting arrangement differed from the basic design, there being three goalpost masts, two forward and one aft, with pole topmasts fitted to the forward and after crossbeams. A special feature of this variation allowed the topmasts to be unshipped, thus permitting the ships to pass under the bridges of the Manchester Ship Canal when on service to the United Kingdom.

Built by Federal SB & DD Co., Kearny, NJ.

MC Hull Nos 67-71 Yard Nos 172-176

172 JOSEPH LYKES 11.40 1958: Marad Reserve, Beaumont, Texas. 2.1972: Scrapped Brownsville, Texas.

JOSEPH LYKES, the first C1-type ship *Skyfotos*

JOSEPH LYKES and ZOELLA LYKES, the first two CI-B ships, laid up — double-banked — at New Orleans
Author's collection

173 ZOELLA LYKES 11.40 11.1943: Completed conversion to a transport (1,444 troops) by Bethlehem Steel Co., 27th Street Yard, New York, for operation by the WSA. 3.1946: Returned to owners. 1958: Marad Reserve, Mobile. 2.1973: Scrapped Panama City.

174 REUBEN TIPTON (I) 12.40 23.10.1942: Sunk by submarine (U.129) torpedo in position 14·33N 54·58W, (NE of Barbados).

FRED MORRIS as the submarine tender OTUS *U.S.N.*

175 FRED MORRIS (I) 12.40 3.1941: Acquired by the US Navy and converted to a submarine tender, renamed OTUS (AS 20). 6.1945: Reclassified as a repair ship (ARG 20). 1946: FRED MORRIS (USMC). 1947: Returned to Lykes. 1948: USMC Reserve, Olympia, Wash., as OTUS (USN). 11.1970. Scrapped Portland, Ore.

176 JOHN LYKES 1.41 12.1943: Completed conversion to a transport (1,288 troops) by the Zalud Marine Corp., New York, for operation by the WSA. 2.1946: Released. 1958: Marad Reserve, Mobile. 12.1972: Scrapped Panama City.

An order for four ships was placed in September 1939, these to be constructed at the Long Beach yard of the Los Angeles Division of the Consolidated Steel Corporation.

The first ship, CAPE MENDOCINO, was the first cargo vessel to be built in Southern California since the World War I shipbuilding programme ended. She was turned over to the New York & Cuba Mail SS Co., and renamed AGWIMONTE, making her first voyage in September 1941. The second ship, AGWIPRINCE, followed two months later. The other ships of the order were taken by the Alcoa SS Co.

MC Hull Nos 75-78 Yard Nos 156-159

156 Laid down as CAPE MENDOCINO (I) 9.41 1941: AGWIMONTE. 29.5.1943: Sunk by submarine (U 177) torpedo in position 34·57S 19·33E, off Cape Agulhas, South Africa.

157 AGWIPRINCE 11.41 2.1944: Completed conversion to a transport (1,223 troops) by Bethlehem Steel Co., 27th Street Yard, New York, for operation by the WSA. 3.1946: USMC Reserve. 3.1965: Scrapped Baltimore.

ALCOA PENNANT in post-war colours *World Ship Photo Library*

158 ALCOA PENNANT 12.41 Intended to become naval cargo ship AK 50 (USN) but not acquired. 5.1965: Scrapped Mobile.

159 ALCOA POLARIS 2.42 1.1944: Completed conversion to a transport (1,163 troops) by Zalud Marine Corp., New York, for operation by the WSA. 3.1946: Returned to owner. 8.1965: Scrapped Panama City.

Also in September 1939, five turbine-driven ships were ordered for Lykes Bros SS Co., three of which were lost during hostilities.

Built by Bethlehem Steel Co., Sparrows Point, Md.

MC Hull Nos 79-83 Yard Nos 4344-4348

JAMES LYKES on the fitting-out berth, in 1940 *U.S.M.C.*

4344 JAMES LYKES 12.40 1958: Marad Reserve, Mobile. 12.1972: Scrapped Panama City.

4345 LIPSCOMB LYKES (I) 2.41 18.1.1943: Wrecked on Durand Reef, SE of Loyalty Islands, New Caledonia.

4346 THOMPSON LYKES 4.41 1958: Marad Reserve, Mobile. 6.1973: Scrapped Panama City.

4347 SOLON TURMAN (I) .41 13.6.1942: Sunk by submarine (U.159) torpedo off Colon, 10·45N 80·24W.

4348 JAMES McKAY .41 8.12.1942: Sunk by submarine (U.600) torpedo in N. Atlantic, 57·50N 23·10W (Voyage New York/Belfast).

THOMPSON LYKES *Skyfotos*

Another order in September 1939 also numbered five turbine-driven ships. The first was handed over to the American Mail Lines, the remainder were for the Alcoa SS Co.

Built by Bethlehem Steel Co., San Francisco, Cal.

MC Hull Nos 84-88 Yard Nos 5360-5364

5360 Laid down as CAPE SAN MARTIN (I) 2.41 Completed as SANTA CRUZ. 11.1943: Completed conversion to a transport (1,128 troops) by Bethlehem Steel Co., Hoboken, for operation by the WSA. 2.1946: USMC Reserve, Suisun Bay. 9.1970: Scrapped Oakland, Cal.

5361 ALCOA PIONEER 3.41 1963: Marad Reserve. 7.1970: Scrapped Valencia.

ALCOA PIONEER, showing a charterer's funnel colours *Author's collection*

ALCOA PILGRIM after trials in July 1941. She was sunk in 1942 *Author's collection*

5362 ALCOA PILGRIM (I) 7.41 27.5.1942: Sunk by submarine (U.558) torpedo in Caribbean Sea, 16·28N 67·37W.

5363 ALCOA PATRIOT 8.41 11.1943: Completed conversion to a transport (1,175 troops) by Arthur Blair Shipyard, New York for operation by the WSA. 1946: Returned to owner. 1963: Marad Reserve. 5.1964: Scrapped USA.

5364 ALCOA PURITAN (I) 9.41 6.5.1942: Sunk by submarine (U.507) torpedo in Gulf of Mexico, 28·35N 88·22W (Voyage Trinidad/Mobile).

ALCOA PATRIOT *World Ship Photo Library*

Built by Bethlehem Steel Co., Staten Island.

Part of the large order for steam turbine ships placed in the summer of 1939, the first two of these five were handed over to the Alcoa SS Co., the next two were operated by the United States Mail SS Co as troopships during the war, whilst the fifth ship was handed over to Lykes Bros SS Co.

MC Hull Nos 89-93 Yard Nos 8015-8019

8015 Laid down as CAPE MAY (I) 1.41 Completed as ALCOA PATHFINDER. 22.11.1942: Sunk by submarine (U.181) torpedo off Portuguese East Africa, 26·45S 33·10E.

8016 Laid down as CAPE ANN (I) 3.41 Completed as ALCOA PROSPECTOR. 5.7.1943: Damaged by Japanese submarine (I.27) torpedo in Arabian Sea, 24·21N 59·04E. Towed to Persian Gulf. Temporarily repaired. 2.1944: Towed to Karachi, thence to Bombay by the Liberty ship JOHN A. POOR. 1945: Returned to USMC in damaged condition. Sold. 1950: Scrapped Philadelphia.

8017 CAPE NEDDICK 5.41 1.1944: Completed conversion to a transport (1,232 troops) by Bethlehem Steel Co., Hoboken, for operation by the WSA. 1947: (USMC). 1965: Scrapped USA.

CAPE COD, whilst operated by the United Fruit Co *World Ship Photo Library*

8018 CAPE COD 6.41 2.1944: Completed conversion to a transport (1,261 troops) by Arthur G. Blair Inc., Yonkers, New York, for operation by the WSA. 1946: Sold commercial (same name). 1964: CAPE TRADER. 7.1968: Scrapped Onomichi.

8019 STELLA LYKES (I) 8.41 27.7.1942: Sunk by submarine (U.582) torpedo in N. Atlantic, 06·40N 25·05W.

Built by Western Pipe & Steel Co., San Francisco, Cal.

These five ships constituted the first order of a rejuvenated yard which had ceased ship construction in 1921, the order being placed in October 1939. The ships were intended for the United States Lines' service across the Atlantic but were switched to the Orient and Australasian run when war broke out in Europe. They were placed under the American Pioneer Line flag.

They were motorships, propelled by two 7-cylinder Busch-Sulzer diesel engines with an electro-magnetic coupling interposed between each engine and the reduction gear. This operated on the same principle as an induction motor.

MC Hull Nos 94-98 Yard Nos 57-61

AMERICAN MANUFACTURER as PRESIDENT OSMENA *Author's collection*

57 AMERICAN MANUFACTURER 4.41 1945: (USMC). 1948: HOEGH MERCHANT. 1956: MATHILDA. 1963: PRESIDENT OSMENA. 1965: SEVEN GENERALS. 1973: Scrapped Kaohsiung.

58 AMERICAN LEADER 6.41 10.9.1942: Sunk by German raider MICHEL (Schiff 28) near St. Helena, S. Atlantic, (Voyage Cape Town/Punta Arenas).

59 AMERICAN BUILDER 7.41 1945: (USMC). 1952: CAPE DECISION. In Reserve, James River. 1968: (US Army).

60 AMERICAN PRESS 9.41 1945: (USMC). 1952: CAPE LOOKOUT. In Reserve, Hudson River. 12.1970: Scrapped Bilbao.

61 AMERICAN PACKER 10.41 1945: (USMC). In Reserve, Hudson River. 6.1971: Scrapped Valencia.

AMERICAN PACKER, on trials in 1941 *Author's collection*

Built by Seattle Tacoma Shipbuilding Corporation (Todd Pacific Shipyard Inc)

These five ships, ordered in October 1939, were motor-driven. Three were operated by the American Mail Line and two others were purchased after launching by the Pacific Atlantic SS Co., of Portland, managers of the States SS Co., for the latter's service between the Columbia River and the Orient. The two ships were renamed OREGON and IDAHO. The IDAHO, launched on 26 June 1941 as CAPE DOUGLAS (I) was the last of the early C1-B type orders by the Maritime Commission.

MC Hull Nos 119-123 Yard Nos 1-5

CAPE ALAVA as WAIRIMU, in New Zealand waters *Author's collection*

1 **CAPE ALAVA 4.41** 1948: WAIRIMU. 1966: TA TUNG 1969: TA TZONG. 3.1970: Scrapped Kaohsiung.

This was the first vessel launched at this yard (1 August 1940) and was the first C1-B motorship.

2 **CAPE FLATTERY 5.41** 1.1943: Completed conversion to a transport (552 troops) at San Francisco, for operation by the WSA. 4.1946: Returned to USMC in damaged condition after engine trouble at New York. Laid up in Reserve, Hudson River. 4.1971: Scrapped Valencia.

3 **Laid down as CAPE CLEAR 8.41** Completed as OREGON. 10.12.1941: In collision, on maiden voyage, off Nantucket, (Voyage Lourenco Marques/Boston). Sank, 41·20N 70·02W.

4 **CAPE FAIRWEATHER 7.41** 1946: In Reserve, James River.

This ship was designed originally as an ore carrier for the Alcoa SS Co but before completion was assigned to the American Mail Line of Seattle to whose plans she was completed. She sailed on her maiden voyage from Vancouver BC to the Far East on 19 July 1941.

5 **Laid down as CAPE DOUGLAS (I) 9.41** Completed as IDAHO. 1951: BRIGHTSTAR. 1954: KRONOS. 14.3.1962: Aground on Kos Island (Dodecanese Islands) (Voyage Skaramanga/Yali Island — ballast). 23.3.1962: Refloated. CTL. 6.1962: Scrapped Spezia.

The American Mail Line

The American Mail Line was formed in 1931, under the Dollar SS Co. It was re-organised early in 1940, the new company arranging discharge from bankruptcy of the old company. In the February a bid was made to charter six old 'Hog Island' cargo ships from the USMC and this was arranged in the following month, the service at first being from Puget Sound to the Orient.

The company then planned to purchase, or charter, three C1 and six C2 type ships from the Maritime Commission. The first C1, CAPE ALAVA, was delivered on 3 April 1941, followed by CAPE FLATTERY on 29 May and CAPE FAIRWEATHER on 8 July.

CAPE ALAVA, the first C1-B motorship *World Ship Photo Library*

Orders for the C2 ships were placed with the Sun yard (yard Nos 199-201) and the Federal SB & DD Co (yard Nos 184-186). The latter however, were purchased by the Mississippi Shipping Company and a further three ships were ordered from the Moore shipyard, scheduled for delivery at the end of 1942 and to be named OREGON MAIL, WASHINGTON MAIL and AMERICAN MAIL.

LATER ORDERS

Built by Consolidated Steel Corp., Wilmington, Cal.

Propelling machinery consists of two steam turbines double reduction geared to a single shaft and developing 4,400 shp.

MC Hull Nos	263-266	Yard Nos	222-225
	486-511		226-251
	698-701		276-279
	1015-1028		331-344
	1042-1044		358-360
	1693-1695		537-539
	2073-2079		752-758

222 MORMACHAWK (II) 12.42 Completed as a transport (1,337 troops) for operation by the WSA. 2.1946: (USMC). 3.1964: Scrapped Portland, Ore.

223 MORMACWREN (II) 12.42 9.1943: Completed conversion to a transport (1,328 troops) at San Francisco for operation by the WSA. 2.1946: (USMC) 2.1965: Scrapped Kearny, NJ.

224 MORMACDOVE (II) 12.42 12.1943: Completed conversion to a transport (1,171 troops) by Todd Shipyard, Hoboken for operation by the WSA. 3.1946: (USMC). 2.1965: Scrapped Kearny, NJ.

225 MORMACGULL (II) 2.43 1946: MORMACREED. 1959: Marad Reserve, James River. 8.1970: Scrapped Spezia.

226 MORMACLARK (II) 2.43 1959: Marad Reserve, James River. 7.1970: Scrapped Bilbao.

227 MORMACTERN 2.43 1959: Marad Reserve, James River. 19.6.1968: Scuttled with cargo of chemical ammunition in position 39.37N 71.01W.

228 NANCY LYKES (II) 2.43 1958: Marad Reserve, Mobile. 4.1972: Scrapped Panama City.

229 JEAN LYKES (II) 2.43 1958: Marad Reserve, Beaumont. 3.1972: Scrapped Brownsville, Texas.

JEAN LYKES *Author's collection*

ALCOA PARTNER as the Navy cargo ship AURIGA, April 1943 *U.S.N.*

230 FRED MORRIS (II) 2.43 4.1944: Completed conversion to a transport (1,575 troops) by Todd Shipyard, Hoboken for operation by the US Navy. Renamed ARLINGTON (AP 174).3.1946: returned to Lykes as FRED MORRIS. 1948: (USMC). 2.1965: Scrapped Baltimore.

231 SOLON TURMAN (II) 2.43 1958: Marad Reserve, Beaumont. 2.1972: Scrapped Brownsville, Texas.

232 ALCOA PLANTER 3.43 31.1.1963: Afire while discharging at Bremen. CTL. 4.1963: Scrapped Hamburg.

233 ALCOA PARTNER 3.43 1943: AURIGA (AK 98) (USN). 1946: ALCOA PARTNER. 1963: (Marad). 7.1970: Scrapped Valencia.

ALCOA PARTNER after post-war conversion from the U.S. Navy ship AURIGA *World Ship Photo Library*

234 ALCOA PILGRIM (II) 3.43 1963: (Marad). 2.1965: Scrapped Mobile.

235 ALCOA PURITAN (II) 3.43 1963: (Marad). 2.1965: Scrapped Mobile.

236 ALCOA POINTER 4.43 1963: (Marad). 12.1966: Scrapped Kearny NJ.

237 ALCOA PEGASUS 4.43 1962: TRANSMARINER. 3.1968: Scrapped Kaohsiung.

ALCOA PEGASUS *Author's collection*

ALCOA PEGASUS as TRANSMARINER. *Author's collection*

CAPE PERPETUA as a troopship *U.S. Army*

238 CAPE TRINITY 5.43 Built at Long Beach yard. In Reserve Beaumont. 6.1972: Scrapped Brownsville, Texas.

239 CAPE SAN MARTIN (II) 4.43 In Reserve, Suisun Bay. 7.1974: Scrapped Portland, Ore.

240 CAPE ROMAIN 4.43 In Reserve, Mobile.12.1975: Scrapped Panama City.

241 CAPE MAY (II) 5.43 In Reserve, Suisun Bay.

242 CAPE NEWENHAM 4.43 12.1943: Completed conversion to a transport (1,830 troops) by Moore DD Co., Oakland for operation by the WSA. 7.1946: In Reserve, Suisun Bay. 3.1965: Scrapped Oakland, Cal.

243 CAPE PERPETUA 5.43 12.1943: Completed conversion to a transport (2,006 troops) by General Eng. & DD. Co., San Francisco for operation by the WSA. 1946: (USMC). 6.1965: Scrapped Oakland, Cal.

244 CAPE CLEARE 5.43 11.1943: Completed conversion to a transport (1,791 troops) by Todd Shipyards, Seattle for operation by the WSA. 1946: (USMC). 5.1965: Scrapped Terminal Island.

CAPE CLEARE *U.S. Army*

CAPE JOHNSON *Consolidated Steel Corp.*

245 CAPE MENDOCINO (II) 6.43 11.1943: Completed conversion to a transport (1,721 troops) by Matson Nav. Co., San Francisco for operation by the WSA. 1946: (USMC). 6.1965: Scrapped Oakland, Cal.

246 CAPE ANN (II) 6.43 1947: sold commercial (same name). 1963: TRANSUNION. 1968: Scrapped Taiwan.

247 CAPE JOHNSON 5.43 6.1944: Completed conversion to a transport (1,575 troops) by Los Angeles SB & DD. Co. Bareboat chartered to US Navy as AP 172. 7.1946: (USMC). 5.1963: Scrapped Portland, Ore.

248 CAPE ELIZABETH 6.43 11.1978: Scrapped Richmond, Cal.

249 CAPE SAN JUAN 6.43

When this ship left the builder's yard as a cargo carrier she was sent immediately for conversion to a transport to carry 1,342 troops for operation by the WSA. These alterations were made at San Francisco between June and August 1943. On her second voyage as a transport from San Francisco, bound for Townsville, Australia, she was near the Fiji Islands, in position 22.08S 178.06E when she was hit by a torpedo from the Japanese submarine I.21 on 11 November 1943. The Liberty ship, EDWIN T. MEREDITH took off several hundred troops while three US Navy ships rescued many more. An attempt was made to tow the badly listing CAPE SAN JUAN after she had been abandoned, but she sank the following day.

CAPE SAN JUAN, torpedoed and sunk in 1943 *U.S. Army*

CAPE MEARES *U.S. Army*

250 CAPE MEARES 6.43 10.1943: Completed conversion to a transport (1,815 troops) by United Engineering Co., San Francisco for operation by the WSA. 1946: released. 7.1965: Scrapped Oakland, Cal.

251 CAPE GREIG 6.43 8.1978: Scrapped Richmond, Cal.

276 CAPE STEPHENS 6.43 In Reserve, Suisun Bay. 7.1974: Scrapped Portland, Ore.

277 CAPE SANDY 7.43 Built at Long Beach yard. 1947: DONA AURORA. 1950: CUANZA. 1950: ELMINA. 1955: NIAS. 1963: TORRES. 1966: AMASIA. 1967: MACASSAR SKY. 3.1970: Scrapped Kaohsiung.

278 CAPE FRIENDSHIP 8.43 Built at Long Beach yard. In Reserve, Hudson River. 9.1970: Scrapped Bilbao.

279 CAPE MEREDITH 9.43 1948: TRINIDAD. 1966: FROSSINI. 5.1969: Scrapped Kaohsiung.

CAPE MEREDITH as TRINIDAD *Author's collection*

331 HOPE 8.43 Completed as US Navy hospital ship HOPE (AH 7). 5.1946: Transferred to US Army. 1949: (USMC). In reserve, Suisun Bay. 1.1975: Sold Houston shipbreakers.

332 CAPE ORANGE 3.44 1947: SIR JOHN FRANKLIN. 1968: TIA MARIA. 4.1970: Scrapped Hong Kong.

Sideways launch of CAPE ORANGE in 1944 *Author's collection*

CAPE ORANGE *World Ship Photo Library*

CAPE ORANGE as SIR JOHN FRANKLIN *Vic Young*

333 CAPE CUMBERLAND 4.44 1948: sold commercial, (same name). 1955: SANTA ANITA. 1966: SANTA VICTORIA. 6.1971: Scrapped Taiwan.

334 CAPE MARTIN 5.44 In Reserve, Suisun Bay. 4.1975: Scrapped Richmond, Cal.

335 CAPE JOHN 5.44 In Reserve, Mobile. 6.1972: Scrapped Mobile.

336 CAPE LAMBERT 6.44 In Reserve, Suisun Bay. 1970: Scrapped Terminal Island.

337 COMFORT 8.43 Completed as US Navy hospital ship COMFORT (AH 6). 4.1946: Transferred to US Army. 1949: (USMC). 1955: STATE OF MAINE (State of Maine Maritime Academy). 10.1967: Scrapped New Orleans.

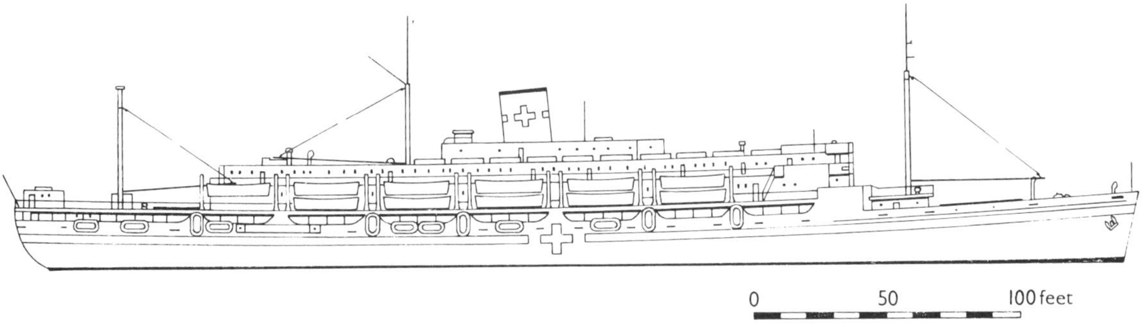

The hospital ship MERCY

338 MERCY 8.43 Completed as US Navy hospital ship MERCY (AH 8) by Los Angeles SB & DD Co., San Pedro, Cal. 5.1946: Transferred to US Army. 1949: (USMC). 1956: EMPIRE STATE III (State University of New York Maritime College). 1960: (Marad). 6.1971: Scrapped Valencia.

339 CAPE GEORGIA 7.43 1949: SHIRLEY LYKES. 1961: Marad Reserve, Beaumont. 3.1972: Scrapped Houston Texas.

340 CAPE CONSTANCE 7.43 1947: DONA TRINIDAD. 25.6.1947: Ashore at Nijo Gan Lighthouse off Sakhalin Island, 45.47N 142.13E (Voyage: Shanghai/Sakhalin-ballast). Abandoned when breaking up.

341 CAPE VICTORY 7.43 2.1944: Completed conversion to a transport (1,319 troops) by Matson Nav. Co., San Francisco, for operation by the WSA. 2.1946: (USMC). 11.1964: Scrapped Tacoma, Wash.

342 CAPE ISABEL 8.43 In Reserve, Wilmington, NC. 3.1968: Scrapped Wilmington, NC.

CAPE DOMINGO *World Ship Photo Library*

343 CAPE ALEXANDER 8.43 1948: AGWIMONTE. 1950: ORIZABA. 1963: PUERTO RICO. 1968: HIGHLAND PARK. 7.1970: Scrapped Kaohsiung.

344 CAPE CHALMERS 8.43 1948: AGWISTAR. 1950: MONTEREY. 1963: Marad Reserve, James River. 4.1971: Scrapped Bilbao.

358 CAPE DOMINGO 2.44 1947: FLYING INDEPENDENT. 1965: HARBOR HILLS. 9.1968: Scrapped Kaohsiung.

359 CAPE KILDARE 3.44 1948: GEORGE LYKES. 1962: (Marad). 1967: CAPE KILDARE. 5.1968: Scrapped Kaohsiung.

360 CAPE KUMUKAKI 3.44 1947: FLYING ENTERPRISE.
(see The FLYING ENTERPRISE Story, page 65)

537 CAPE CATOCHE 3.44 9.1969: Loaded with obsolete ammunition and scuttled off USA.

538 CAPE ARCHWAY 3.44 1949: BRINTON LYKES. 1961: (Marad). 1967: CAPE ARCHWAY. In Reserve, Suisun Bay. 8.1974: Sold to California shipbreakers.

539 CAPE SAUNDERS 8.44 1.1970: Scrapped Hirao.

752 CAPE LILIBEO 3.44 1947: FRED MORRIS. 1961: Marad Reserve, Suisun Bay.

CAPE TRYON as ADABELLE LYKES *John G. Callis*

753 CAPE TRYON 4.44 1947: ADABELLE LYKES. 1962: (Marad). 1966: CAPE TRYON. In Reserve, Suisun Bay. 1969: Loaded with obsolete ammunition and 12.8.1969: scuttled 90 miles off Cape Flattery, 48.15N 127.00W.

754 CAPE POSSESSION 5.44 1949: MARION LYKES. 1961: Marad Reserve, Beaumont. 12.1971: Scrapped Houston, Texas.

755 CAPE JUNCTION 4.44 2.1970: Scrapped Sakaide.

756 CAPE SAN DIEGO 8.44 9.1978: Scrapped Richmond, Cal.

757 CAPE EDMONT 9.44 In Reserve, Suisun Bay.

758 CAPE SPEAR 11.44 1948: AGWIPRINCESS. 1951: MEXICO. 1954: SANTA FE. 9.1971: Scrapped Kaohsiung.

Built by Consolidated Steel Corp. Wilmington, Cal. **C1-S-AY1 type**

MC Hull Nos 1029-1041 Yard Nos 345-357

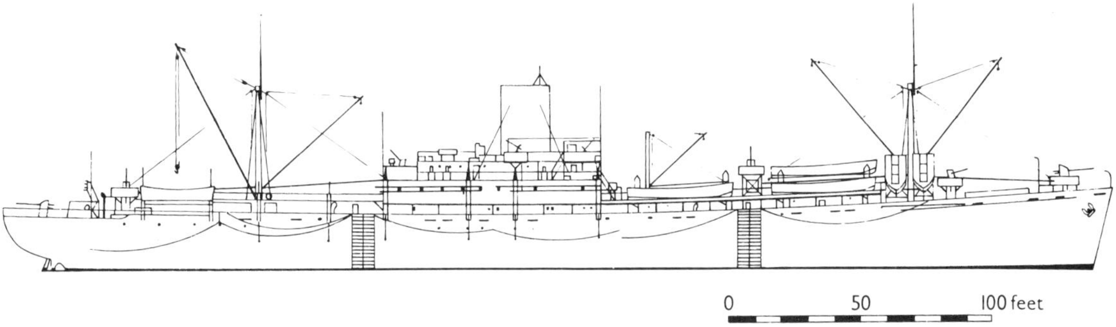

Landing Ship Infantry (Large)-the C1-S-AY1 type

345 **Laid down as CAPE BERKELEY 10.43** Completed as EMPIRE BATTLEAXE. 1946: DONOVAN (RN) (F 161). 6.1946: EMPIRE BATTLEAXE. 1947: (USMC). 1948: CAPE BERKELEY. 1948: to be sold to China as HAI C, but sale cancelled. 1948: EMPIRE BATTLEAXE. 5.1966: Scrapped Kearny, NJ.

346 **Laid down as CAPE COMPASS 11.43** Completed as EMPIRE CUTLASS. 1945: SANSOVINO (RN) (F162). 6.1946: EMPIRE CUTLASS. 1947: (USMC). 1948: CAPE COMPASS. 1948: to be sold to China as HAI OU, but sale postponed. 1948: EMPIRE CUTLASS. 1960: HAI OU. 10.1970: Scrapped Kaohsiung.

CAPE COMPASS rebuilt as the Chinese HAI OU, in Eastern waters. *Airfoto, Malacca*

347 Laid down as CAPE GREGORY 11.43 Completed as EMPIRE HALBERD. 1944: SILVIO (RN) (F160). 1945: EMPIRE HALBERD. 1948: (USMC). 1948: CAPE GREGORY. 12.1966: Scrapped at Baltimore as IMPERIAL HALBERD.

348 Laid down as CAPE MARSHALL 12.43 Completed as EMPIRE BROADSWORD. 2.7.1944: Mined and sunk in English Channel, 49.25N 00.54W.

349 Laid down as CAPE PINE 12.43 Completed as EMPIRE LANCE. 1945: SIR HUGO (RN). 1945: EMPIRE LANCE. 1949: CAPE PINE. 12.1966: Scrapped at Baltimore as IMPERIAL LANCE.

350 Laid down as CAPE ST ROQUE 12.43 Completed as EMPIRE MACE. 1944: GALTEEMORE (RN) (F 171). 1947: MISR.

Owned by the Government of Egypt and used as a transport etc, this vessel was one of the first three commercial ships to transit the Suez Canal in November 1974 since its closure in June 1967. The three vessels (including the SYRIA and ASWAN STAR) carried pilgrims to Saudi Arabia, bound for the Moslem holy city of Mecca. The same three ships were used in the reverse direction in May 1975 to simulate a convoy of fifteen (some real and others imaginary) ships which left Suez City for Port Said to train pilots prior to the opening of the Canal on 5 June 1975.

351 Laid down as CAPE TURNER 12.43 Completed as EMPIRE RAPIER. 1948: (USMC). 1948: CAPE TURNER. 5.1966: Scrapped Kearny, NJ., as EMPIRE RAPIER.

CAPE COMORIN as the Infantry Landing ship SEFTON, in 1946 *Wright & Logan*

CAPE ST. VINCENT as the Egyptian transport AL SUDAN, at Cape Town *Vic Young*

352 Laid down as CAPE ARGOS 1.44 Completed as EMPIRE ANVIL. 1944: ROCKSAND (RN) (F 184). 6.1946: EMPIRE ANVIL. 1947: (USMC). 1948: CAPE ARGOS. 1948: To be sold to China as HAI YA, but sale postponed. 1948: EMPIRE ANVIL. 1960: HAI YA. 1973: FU MING. 1974: Scrapped China.

353 Laid down as CAPE LOBOS 1.44 Completed as EMPIRE JAVELIN. 28.12.1944: Sunk by submarine (U.772) torpedo in English Channel, in position 50.05N 01.00W.

354 Laid down as CAPE GIRARDEAU 1.44 Completed as EMPIRE SPEARHEAD. 1947: (USMC). 1948: CAPE GIRARDEAU. 1948: To be sold to China as HAI MEI, but sale cancelled. 1951: EMPIRE SPEARHEAD. 11.1966: Scrapped Baltimore.

355 Laid down as CAPE ST. VINCENT 1.44 Completed as EMPIRE ARQUEBUS. 1945: CICERO (RN) (F 170). 1946: EMPIRE ARQUEBUS. 1947: AL SUDAN.

356 Laid down as CAPE COMORIN 1.44 Completed as EMPIRE GAUNTLET. 1944: SEFTON (RN) (F 123). 9.1946: EMPIRE GAUNTLET. 1947: CAPE COMORIN. 12.1964: Scrapped Portsmouth, Va.

357 Laid down as CAPE WASHINGTON 1.44 Completed as EMPIRE CROSSBOW. 1944: SAINFOIN (RN) (F 183). 9.1946: EMPIRE CROSSBOW. 1947: (USMC). 1947: CAPE WASHINGTON. 12.1964: Scrapped Portsmouth, Va.

The Consolidated Steel Corporation

The Consolidated Steel Corporation was formed in 1928, three leading iron works in Los Angeles — the Llewellyn Iron Works, Baker Iron Works and Union Iron Works forming an amalgamation of interests in structural steelwork, industrial buildings, bridges etc. Two years later a new plant was built at Maywood just east of the city.

When the Maritime Commission came into operation in 1936 and announced its ten-year programme, the Consolidated Corporation leased an old shipyard at Long Beach, some 20 miles south of Los Angeles, bid for and was awarded a contract for the construction of four C1 type vessels (Yard Nos 156-9). The shipyard however, had only one way and that built parallel to the channel, so that only sideways launchings could be made. However, there was room on the way to build an additional half a ship so that when the complete ship was launched, the second half of the partly completed ship was commenced and another half started. The first vessel, AGWIMONTE, launched on 14 November 1940 was the first cargo ship to be built in southern California since the World War I programme had ceased.

CAPE MENDOCINO as AGWIMONTE, on trials. She was sunk in 1943 *Author's collection*

During the ensuing war years, several more C1 cargo ships were constructed at Long Beach, plus the P1 transports DOYEN and FELAND in 1943 and some coastwise cargo ships of the C1-M-AV1 type.

On 2 August 1941, the Corporation put the first of some 40,000 piles into reclaimed mudland at Wilmington, some 20 miles south of Los Angeles, to begin an eight-way yard. With its ancillary buildings this was to cover some 95 acres with over a mile of quayage. The first ship of a thirty C1-ship contract (Yard Nos 222-251) was laid on 1 December 1941 and was launched on 11 May 1942 as the MORMACHAWK. Indeed, the yard had keels down and hull construction in progress on each way as the way was completed.

Both shipyards were fed from the parent plant at Mayfield, which had been adapted to manufacture the plating and fabricated sections of the ships, transporting them by rail to the shipyards for erection.

The Wilmington yard went on to build a large class of attack transports of the S4-SE2-BD1 type, eighteen frigates which were built under US Maritime Commission jurisdiction and turned over to the US Navy on completion and ten C2 type vessels in 1946. Thirteen C1 ships were converted before completion as landing ships for Britain as well as three hospital ships for the US Navy which were delivered to the Navy the same day as each was launched.

The Consolidated Steel Corporation also had a wholly-owned subsidiary company at Orange, Texas — the Consolidated Steel Corporation of Texas, with an adjacent shipbuilding division which built many destroyers for the US Navy.

The first early orders for C1-A shelterdeck ships were given in October 1939 when Pennsylvania Shipyards Inc., of Beaumont were contracted to build two ships for delivery in 1941. Both ships were motor vessels, the first, CAPE LOOKOUT being taken over before completion and modified as an attack cargo ship for the US Navy. The second ship was for Moore-McCormack Lines. The yard went on to build another forty-four diesel engined ships for the United States Maritime Commission in four bulk contracts.

MC Hull Nos	138-139	Yard Nos	227-228
	223-232		256-265
	688-697		266-275
	1284-1303		284-303
	1961-1964		313-316

227 Laid down as CAPE LOOKOUT (I) 5.41 Completed as FOMALHAUT (AK 22). 1943: Reclassed (AKA 5). 1944: Reclassed (AK 22). 1948: Reclassed (AE 20). 1962: To Marad Reserve, Hudson River. 1.1972: Scrapped Baltimore.

228 MORMACDALE 2.42 1959: Marad Reserve, James River. 2.1975: Scrapped Philadelphia.

256 CAPE ROMANO 7.42 1947: DEL CAMPO. 1969: OAKDALE. 10.1969: Scrapped Kaohsiung.

257 CAPE ST GEORGE 7.42 1946: RAVNANGER. 1962: NOPAL VERDE. 1966: SUBIC BAY. 10.1973: Scrapped Kaohsiung.

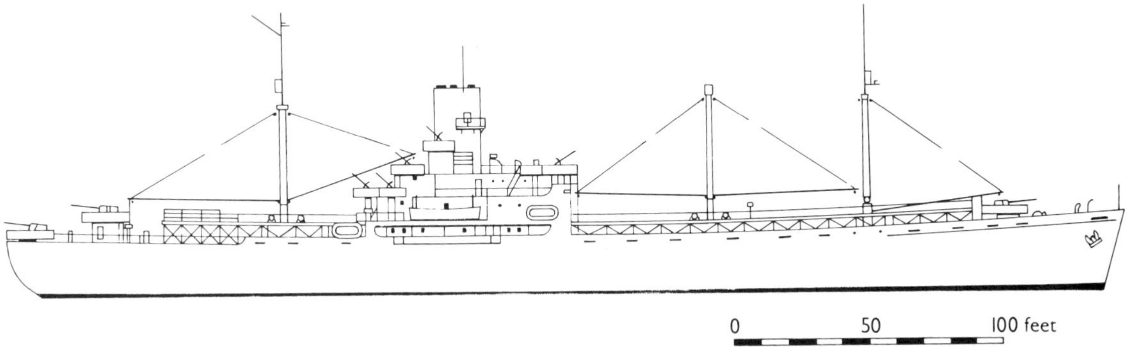

The ammunition ship SANGAY

258 Laid down as CAPE SABLE (I) 9.42 Completed as SANGAY (AE 10). 1947: To USN Reserve. 1960: To Marad Reserve, Beaumont.

259 CAPE PORPOISE 9.42 1946: BOWHILL. 1955: SUNHILL. 1967: SPETSAI. 4.1969: Scrapped Kaohsiung.

260 CAPE HENRY 10.42 1947: DEL VIENTO. 1959: Marad Reserve, Mobile. 7.1973: Scrapped Panama City.

261 CAPE DECISION 11.42 27.1.1943: sunk by submarine (U.105) torpedo in North Atlantic, 22.57N 47.28W.

CAPE SPENCER as PRESIDENT ROXAS *Author's collection*

262 CAPE SPENCER 12.42 1947: ELIN HORN. 1963: PRESIDENT ROXAS. 1973: LUCKY SEVEN. 9.1973: Scrapped Kaohsiung.

263 CAPE ST ELIAS 12.42 1947: BOWRIO. 1953: NOPAL BRANCO. 1967: DINGALAN BAY. 9.1973: Scrapped Kaohsiung.

264 CAPE UGAT 12.42 1947: PAULA DAN. 1962: REBEVERETT. 1965: REB. 7.1970: Scrapped Mihara.

265 CAPE CANAVERAL 1.43 1946: OLUF MAERSK. 1959: RUTHEVERETT. 1965: RUTH. 11.1971: Scrapped Kaohsiung.

266 CAPE LOOKOUT (II) 3.43 1947: CORNELIUS MAERSK. 1960: DOLPHEVERETT. 1965: RAY. 10.1969: Scrapped Japan.

267 CAPE HATTERAS 3.43 1947: DEL RIO. 1959: Marad Reserve, Beaumont. 8.1971: Scrapped Brownsville, Texas.

268 CAPE ARAGO 4.43 1943: GENERAL RUGE (bareboat charter to Norwegian Government). 1946: BELGRANO. 1961: STROM GUNHILD. 1968: ILIGAN BAY. 24.1.1971: Last reported from position 120 miles NNE of Cabo Villano with leaks due to heavy weather. No further trace, presumed sunk (Voyage: Antwerp/Manila-general and chemicals).

CAPE ARAGO as ILIGAN BAY, off Dover in April 1969 *Skyfotos*

CAPE BARNABAS as TORTUGAS *Skyfotos*

269 CAPE BARNABAS 4.43 1943: GENERAL FLEISCHER (bareboat charter to Norwegian Government). 1946: TORTUGAS. 1967: EMILIO AGUINALDO. 1967: PRESIDENT LAUREL. 1975: LUCKY NINE. 10.1975: Scrapped Kaohsiung.

270 CAPE BLANCO 5.43 1947: BRA-KAR. 1961: TORO. 1967: EASTERN SATURN. 6.1974: Scrapped Kaohsiung.

271 CAPE CONSTANTINE 6.43 1946: HINDANGER. 1961: TAMPA. 1967: MANUEL QUEZON. 1968: PRESIDENT QUIRINO. 1975: LUCKY EIGHT. 5.1975: Scrapped Kaohsiung.

272 CAPE FEAR 6.43 1947: sold commercial, (same name). 1948: K.C. ROGENAES. 1964: SUNRELL. 1968: SOLMICH. 7.1971: Scrapped Taiwan.

CAPE FEAR as SOLMICH *Airfoto, Malacca*

273 CAPE FLORIDA 7.43 1947: SKAUBO. 1955: SUNPRINCESS. 4.1968: Scrapped Kaohsiung.

274 CAPE SAN BLAS 7.43 1947: KIM. 1956: SUNFLOWER. 1.1968: Scrapped Kaohsiung.

275 CAPE IGVAK 8.43 1947: WAIRATA. 1967: SUCCESSFUL DAY. 10.1972: Scrapped Kaohsiung.

CAPE SABLE as the Dutch-flag FORT NASSAU. *World Ship Photo Library*

CAPE SABLE as DELFT *Author's collection*

284 CAPE SABLE (II) 10.43 1943: FORT NASSAU (bareboat chartered to Royal Netherlands Government). 1946: DELFT. 1967: CAMINA BAY. 1968: TIA JUANA. 2.1970: Scrapped Hong Kong.

CAPE NORTH as ALF LINDEBERG *World Ship Photo Library*

285 CAPE NORTH 10.43 1943: ALF LINDEBERG (bareboat chartered to Norwegian Government). 1947: sold commercial, (same name). 1954: SUNROSE. 1962: STROM FOREST. 1970: RYTTERHOLM. 2.1972: Scrapped Whampoa.

286 CAPE PILLAR 10.43 1947: SYGNA. 1966: MANILA BAY. 11.1973: Scrapped Kaohsiung.

CAPE POGE as STOCKHOLT *World Ship Photo Library*

287 CAPE POGE 11.43 1947: STOCKHOLT. 1960: HERLAND. 1964: CONCORDIA HERLAND. 1964: EASTERN VENUS. 1.1973: Scrapped Kaohsiung.

288 CAPE SAN LUCAS 11.43 1947: CONGOSTROOM. 1956: NANUSA. 1963: PRESIDENT AGUINALDO. 1973: LUCKY VI. 4.1977: Scrapped Karachi.

289 CAPE SAN ANTONIO 12.43 1947: NYHAUG. 1955: CONCORDIA CAPO. 12.1972: Scrapped Shanghai.

CAPE PALMAS as FERNCAPE, with 'Alcoa' funnel markings *Author's collection*

290 CAPE PALMAS 12.43 1947: FERNCAPE. 1960: RANBORG. 3.1970: Scrapped Hong Kong.

291 CAPE RIVER 1.44 1944: NARVIK (Bareboat chartered to Norwegian Government). 1946: SIRANGER. 1959: NORTEMAR. 3.1978: Scrapped Karachi.

292 CAPE MATAPAN 2.44 1947: MARNA DAN. 1962: BRADEVERETT. 6.1970: Scrapped Mihara.

293 CAPE LOPEZ 2.44 1947: FRIERFJORD. 1970: RYTTERSUND. 1.1972: Scrapped Shanghai.

294 CAPE JUBY 3.44 1947: DEL SOL. 1959: Marad Reserve, Mobile. 9.1973: Scrapped Panama City.

295 CAPE TRAFALGAR 4.44 1947: HOEGH TRADER. 1958: TENNA DAN. 1963: NOREVERETT. 1965: LEONOR. 1971: Scrapped Onomichi.

296 CAPE FARO 4.44 1947: CRUX. 1954: GREY MASTER. 1960: SIREDAL. 1963: SUNFALCON. 1968: CONCORDIO FALCO. 1968: SOL TULLA. 1968: SCANDIA FALCON. 2.1973: Scrapped Kaohsiung.

CAPE FARO as SUNFALCON *Author's collection*

CAPE BARROW *World Ship Photo Library*

297 CAPE BARROW 5.44 1947: JOHANNES MAERSK. 1949: GOOILAND. 1968: CAPTAIN PAPIS. 1974: STAR OF KAMAL. 1974: AZIZI. 9.1975: Scrapped Karachi.

298 CAPE DUCATO 6.44 1947: LA ESTANCIA. 1952: MONTCALM. 1957: TYR. 1967: EASTERN MARS. 4.1975: Scrapped Hong Kong.

299 CAPE GASPE 6.44 1947: GERDA DAN. 1961: TYSLA. 1964: VIKSFJORD. 1968: RYTTERVIK. 1.1972: Scrapped Shanghai.

CAPE GASPE *World Ship Photo Library*

300 CAPE FRIO 7.44 1947: ARNOLD MAERSK. 1959: DONEVERETT. 1963: DONALD. 28.12.1964: Aground, mouth of Bislig Bay, Mindanao. 19.5.1965: Refloated. CTL. Towed Kaohsiung for scrapping.

301 CAPE NUN 7.44 1947: BOWMONTE. 1953: converted to a liquid chemical carrier at Kiel. Renamed GASBRAS NORTE. 1961: MUNDOGAS NORTE. 1971: Engines removed, used as storeship.

CAPE SEBASTIAN as SOLSYN *Vic Young*

302 CAPE SEBASTIAN 8.44 1947: EIDANGER. 1966: SOLSYN. 1971: GOODYEAR.

303 CAPE FALCON 9.44 1947: GRENANGER. 1962: HERBJORN. 1966: GALVESTON MERCHANT. 1968: INDONESIAN STAR. 26.2.1968: Arrived New York with engine trouble sustained during voyage Tegal/Houston. 8.9.1969: arrived in tow at Cadiz for scrapping.

CAPE BOYER as BOWPLATE *World Ship Photo Library*

313 CAPE BOYER 10.44 1946: BOWPLATE. 1954: SUNBEAM. 1965: GERMONT. 2.1969: Scrapping Kaohsiung.

314 CAPE TEXAS 10.44 1947: DEL ORO. 1961: DEL MONTE. 1968: AMICUS II. 10.1969: Scrapped Kaohsiung.

CAPE PEMBROKE *World Ship Photo Library*

CAPE PEMBROKE as HAV *World Ship Photo Library*

315 CAPE PEMBROKE 11.44 1947: HAV. 1956: HEDDA DAN. 1963: ROSSEVERETT. 1965: ROSS. 2.1971: Scrapped Hiroshima.

316 CAPE BEALE 12.44 1946: HORDA. 1954: SUNLAND. 1966: ELENA. 6.1973: Scrapped Shanghai.

Built by Pusey & Jones Corporation, Wilmington, Del

Early orders for this builder were for two steam turbine driven shelterdeckers, the contract being awarded in November 1939. The first ship, MARINA, was for A. H. Bull & Company, the second for Lykes Bros. Apart from these two vessels, a further seventeen C1-A type ships were built by Pusey & Jones Corporation.

MC Hull Nos		Yard Nos	
	140-141		1075-1076
	296-305		1084-1093
	891-894		1095-1098
	1691-1692		1100-1101
	2556		1107

1075 MARINA 1.42 16.1.1945: Struck mine at Le Havre. Beached and refloated. Towed to US. CTL. Scrapped Philadelphia.

ADABELLE LYKES as a troop transport *U.S. Army*

1076 ADABELLE LYKES 3.42 2.1944: Completed conversion to a transport (1,329 troops) by Eureka SB Corp., New York for operation by the WSA. 1944: (USMC) Laid up pending repairs. 5.1946: returned to owner. 1946: (USMC) Reserve. 2.1965: Scrapped Baltimore.

1084 CAPE HENLOPEN 9.42 1.1944: Completed conversion to a transport (1,232 troops) by McNulty Shipyard, New York for operation by the WSA. 3.1946: USMC Reserve, James River. 2.1965: Scrapped Baltimore.

1085 CAPE MOHICAN 10.42 1947: sold commercial, (same name). 1951: YUCATAN. 1954: SANTA ANITA. 1954: SANTA CRUZ. 1961: (Marad). 9.1970: Scrapped U.S.A.

1086 CAPE CHARLES 12.42 In Reserve, Hudson River. 2.1971: Scrapped Castellon.

1087 CAPE CORWIN 3.43 In Reserve, Mobile. 7.1974: Scrapped Panama City.

Sideways launch of CAPE DOUGLAS. *U.S.M.C.*

1088 CAPE DOUGLAS (II) 4.43 1.1944: Completed conversion to a transport (1,257 troops) by Cardinal Engineering, New York for operation by the WSA. 3.1946: released. 1947: to Ministry of Transport, Great Britain on bareboat charter. 1948: (USMC) Reserve. 11.1964: Scrapped Chesapeake, Va.

1089 CAPE BON 6.43 12.1943: Completed conversion to a transport (1,172 troops) by Bethlehem Steel Co., 56th Street Yard, New York for operation by the WSA. 1946: released. 5.1965: Scrapped Terminal Island.

1090 CAPE BRETON 8.43 In Reserve, Hudson River. 2.1971: Scrapped Castellon.

1091 CAPE CANSO 10.43 2.1944: Completed conversion to a transport (1,300 troops) by A. Tickle Eng. Co., New York for operation by the WSA. 3.1946: USMC Reserve, Suisun Bay. 8.1974: sold to California shipbreakers.

1092 CAPE CARTHAGE 12.43 1944: Converted to a motor torpedo boat tender for the US Navy. Renamed ACONTIUS (AGP 12). 1946: CAPE CARTHAGE (USMC). 1965: reported scrapped Oakland, Cal.

1093 CAPE DIAMOND 2.44

The need for a vessel capable of carrying liquefied petroleum gas had been apparent for some time to the Warren Petroleum Corp of Tulsa, Oklahoma when they approached Pennsylvania Shipyards Inc., at Beaumont, Texas to design such a craft. From the ensuing conversion plans and subsequent purchase of the CAPE DIAMOND in 1946 came the world's first ship devoted entirely to the carrying of liquid petroleum gas.

There were many difficulties to overcome in conversion, for the rules governing the construction and inspection of vessels did not, at that time, incorporate a liquid gas carrier that would carry petroleum gas in large pressure vessels permanently installed. Careful planning had to be made therefore, to install tanks more than 50 feet long and over 50 tons each in weight. A great deal of piping had also to be fitted for the loading and discharge of the tanks. Altogether 68 tanks were fitted in vertical positions ranging from 8 feet to 13 feet in diameter and 25 feet to 48 feet in length. They were stress relieved, all welds tested with magnetic powder, and welds in places over 1 $\frac{3}{8}$th inches in thickness were X-rayed. They were constructed as unfired pressure vessels for a maximum working pressure of 250 p.s.i.g at a maximum temperature of 115°F. The liquid cargo capacity of the ship was 38,053 barrels.

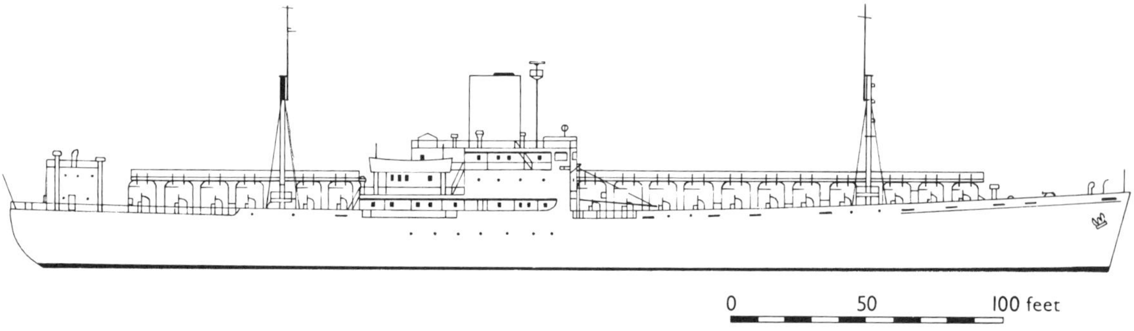

The liquid-gas tanker NATALIE O. WARREN

After a five months conversion ending in November 1947, she sailed regularly under her new name of NATALIE O. WARREN from Houston to New York for the Warren Petroleum Corp., until sold to Oivind Lorentzen in 1961 who worked her in the West Indies-Curacao-East coast of South America trade under the name MUNDOGAS WEST until the end of 1966.

On 15 January 1967 she arrived at Vigo for breaking up but then moved to Santander for scrapping where she arrived on 30 June 1967.

1095 Launched as CAPE FAREWELL 4.44 Completed as CYRENE (AGP 13), a motor torpedo boat tender for the US Navy. 1946: CAPE FAREWELL. USMC Reserve, Suisun Bay. 11.1978: Scrapped Portland, Ore.

1096 CAPE HORN 6.44 In Reserve, Beaumont, Texas. 1971: Scrapped Brownsville, Texas.

1097 CAPE NOME 8.44 1947: sold commercial (same name). 1951: FLYING SPRAY. 1968: TIA PEPITA. 2.1970: Scrapped Hong Kong.

CAPE RACE *World Ship Photo Library*

1098 CAPE RACE 10.44 1947: sold commercial, (same name). 1951: FLYING FOAM. 1959: TRANSBORINQUEN. 2.1970: Scrapped Kaohsiung.

1100 CAPE BORDA 11.44 1947: DEL MONTE. 1959: Marad Reserve, Beaumont. 1.1972: Scrapped New Orleans.

CAPE AVINOFF after removal of wartime armament. *World Ship Photo Library*

1101 CAPE AVINOFF 1.45 1955: TROPICANA.

The CAPE AVINOFF joined the Munargo Line Co., a subsidiary of the United Fruit Co., in 1947.

In 1955 she was bought by the newly-formed Fruit Industries Inc., of Bradenton, Fla., and was equipped with specially designed stainless steel tanks for the carrying of fresh orange juice from the company's processing and storage plant at Merritt Island, near Cocoa, Fla., to New York.

The tanks, fabricated ashore and welded on board because of their size, were insulated with $6\frac{1}{2}$ inches of foam-glass to maintain the orange juice at 28° — 30°F during the voyage. The capacity of the tanks varied from 30,000 to 90,000 gallons.

At New York the juice was pumped ashore into stainless steel tanks at the same temperature.

The ship was renamed TROPICANA after the name of the company's branded orange juice.

In 1958 the company became known as Tropicana Products Inc.

The last voyage of the TROPICANA in this trade was in 1961 when she arrived at New York on 7 June and was laid up. Over a year later, on 14 July she left New York in tow for Tampa and was sold to the Liberian-flag concern Ganaderos del Mar S.A. for general tramping. She was renamed KYRIOS STELIOS under the Liberian flag.

On a voyage from Rostock to Amsterdam she collided with the AZADEH (3,000 grt, 1947) in the Elbe Estuary on 13 June 1966. Beached and then refloated, she was towed to Amsterdam on 17 June 1966 but repairs being uneconomic she was sold to German buyers who resold her to Spanish breakers. Early in September 1966 she arrived at Santander in tow of the tug CINTRA to be broken up.

CAPE AVINOFF as KYRIOS STELIOS, in the English Channel in 1966, just prior to the casualty which led to her scrapping *Skyfotos*

CAPE COMFORT *World Ship Photo Library*

CAPE COMFORT, another view. Note sideports as fitted to some CI vessels *World Ship Photo Library*

1107 CAPE COMFORT 5.45 In Reserve, Olympia, Wash. 6.1970: Transferred to US Navy and 8.1970: Scuttled in Atlantic, off U.S. coast, with obsolete ammunition.

The **FLYING ENTERPRISE** story

The casualty involving the loss of the FLYING ENTERPRISE has become an epic of the sea and the heroic attempts of her master and the attendant salvage ship to save her attracted the floodlight of world publicity, perhaps not so much for the ship, but because of the human interest that stirred the imagination with the valiant efforts to get her to port.

The FLYING ENTERPRISE (ex CAPE KUMUKAKI), owned by the Isbrandtsen Co Inc., of New York was purchased in 1947 from the United States Maritime Commission. She left Hamburg on 21 December 1951 bound for New York with ten passengers and a general cargo which included 1,271 tons of pig iron and 890 tons of African coffee loaded at Rotterdam.

There had been a long series of gales in the Western Approaches at that time and at 12.53 pm on Friday 28 December, Land's End radio received an XXX (urgency signal) from the FLYING ENTERPRISE reporting that she was encountering a severe cyclonic storm (Force 12), some 500 miles west of Fastnet in position 49.20N 17.20W. She stated she had a 30° list to port, a crack across the deck and down each side to the 'tween deck line and was just drifting.

The nearest vessel, the British motorship SHERBORNE (4,986 grt, 1950) radioed at 3.16 pm that she would be with the FLYING ENTERPRISE in six hours. Just sixteen minutes later, at 3.32 pm the FLYING ENTERPRISE gave out an SOS signal. At 7 pm the SHERBORNE was near the scene with the SOUTHLAND (8,186 grt 1944 — a C2-type vessel of the South Atlantic SS Co) and a little later, the Dutch liner NOORDAM (10,726 grt, 1938) arrived, all ships standing by during the night. On the following day, the 29th, the US Navy troopship GENERAL A.W. GREELY (C4-type) was also in the vicinity as was the Waterman SS Co's WAR HAWK (6,135 grt, 1943 — C2-E type).

At 11.30 am the SOUTHLAND went alongside the listing ship and took off seven passengers and eight crew and proceeded on her way to Rotterdam, later reporting she had lost half of her deck load, a complete gangway, a starboard lifeboat and had extensive damage to rails. The GENERAL A. W. GREELY then took off the remaining survivors except the Master, Captain Carlsen and stood by the FLYING ENTERPRISE, which was now listing 60° and rolling to 80° in worsening weather, to await the arrival of a salvage tug. All other vessels proceeded on their respective ways.

The day of the 30th passed and on New Year's Eve there was no change except that the Admiralty tug, TURMOIL (1,136 grt, 1945) on charter to the Overseas Towage & Salvage Co was engaged on a "no cure-no pay" Lloyds Form of Salvage Agreement.

On 2 January the US destroyer JOHN W. WEEKS reached the disabled ship, relieving the US Navy supply ship GOLDEN EAGLE (6,180 grt, 1943 — C2 type) which had arrived and had been standing by. The sea was still rough with a 40 knot WSW wind. The Master of the FLYING ENTERPRISE had now spent four nights alone on his battered ship. The port side and main deck were awash in the heavy swell, No 3 hold was flooded and water had penetrated to the engine room.

The salvage tug TURMOIL left Falmouth at 2 pm on 2 January and reached the FLYING ENTERPRISE, then some 360 miles from Land's End the next night. On 4 January, several attempts were made to connect the FLYING ENTERPRISE. The screw and rudder were now clear of the water and it was found impossible to do this without men on board, for the Master on the FLYING ENTERPRISE could not haul in a heaving line owing to the necessity of holding on with one hand due to the angle of the list.

Later in the day, in even worsening weather and after five attempts to put a line aboard, the Mate of the TURMOIL managed to scramble on board the FLYING ENTERPRISE over the taffrail. The wind had now increased to Force 7, with fog closing in. Finally, at 9.37 am on 5 January a connection was made and the tow started for Falmouth in a moderate sea, at 3 knots with the stricken vessel listing some 40-50° to port, rolling at times to 70°. The towing line was 750 yards long.

By the 6th, with only a slight sea and moderate westerly swells, the FLYING ENTERPRISE, yawing 40°, was in position 48.41N 9.17W. The destroyer JOHN W. WEEKS which had been standing by was relieved by the destroyer WILLARD KEITH. On the 7th, the position at 6 pm was 49.4N 7.37W in a heavy swell.

At the same time the following day the weather had deteriorated and the tow hove to in position 49.26N 6.10W. With an improvement in conditions the tow commenced again at 11.20 am on the 8th but at 1.30 am on the 9th the tow parted and the FLYING ENTERPRISE began to drift with the wind. The conditions were such that it was thought advisable to await daylight before attempting to reconnect.

FLYING ENTERPRISE, shortly before sinking *Shipbuilding & Shipping Record*

Dawn on the 9th gave visibility of 7 miles with a 20 knot WSW wind and 20ft swells, the position being 49.33N 5.31W with the TURMOIL close off the bow of the FLYING ENTERPRISE. The two men aboard were striving to cut the main cable damaged during the night but the ship was rolling 80° to port and pitching, with spray breaking over the bow and the attempts were abandoned. The top deck was now awash on the port side and the ship was drifting away from land. Further attempts were made to re-rig in the afternoon but they also failed, the two men almost being swept into the sea.

At 4 am on the 10th the position was unchanged, the ship 30 miles off the Lizard in rough seas of 9 ft swells. By daylight the westerly gales were still blowing, the FLYING ENTERPRISE slightly deeper, the position 49.35N 4.32W.

In the afternoon the seas were still rough with heavy westerly swells and winds up to 38 knots. The ship was now rolling 85°, the funnel actually slapping the water. There was now no hope of saving the ship. The two men clawed their way to near the funnel but at 3.25 pm hope was abandoned and they jumped into the sea, being quickly hauled on board the TURMOIL. At 3.30 pm the FLYING ENTERPRISE was flat on her side, the bow under the water. Half an hour later only the starboard bow showed and at 4.12 pm she finally sank, about 62 miles from Falmouth, in the position 49.38N 4.23W.

So the FLYING ENTERPRISE did not reach port, but the example of devotion to duty set by her Master, Captain Henrik Kurt Carlsen will endure as will the heroic assistance rendered, in vain, by First Officer Kenneth Roger Dancy, Mate of the TURMOIL.

The C1-M types

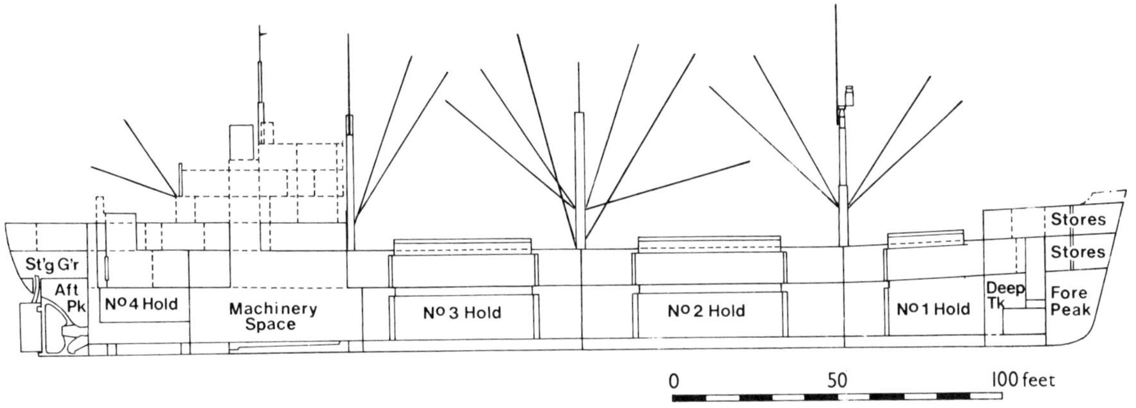

TYPICAL C1-M CARGO VESSEL

Comparisons between 1943 and 1944 shipbuilding production showed just how much output was lost by the interruption of a shipyard's continuity in producing a single type of ship. Nevertheless it was often necessary to make changes even when they immediately indicated that schedules of deliveries would not be met. One reason was a perceptible ease-off after the record breaking production year of 1943 and another the thought that the war might be nearing its end — at least in Europe. But in the Pacific it was another story, for after initial movement of troops and material to secure bases, subsequent movement was still a problem. No general movement could be made by land in the advance toward Japan, but had to take place by the slow re-occupation of hundreds of islands.

A new type of short sea, small, inter-island vessel with shallow draught and able to enter the smaller harbours inaccessible to the bigger transports was therefore required.

Construction of minor types of ships — coastal cargo vessels, tugs and barges — became part of the Maritime Commission's programme during their third wave of expansion and specific additions were made from time to time. Thus a new type, designated C1-M-AV1, was added. Designed to meet the needs of future U.S. Navy operations in the Pacific, it was also to Commission specifications, ensuring that the ships would become permanent units of the post war merchant marine.

Initial orders were placed for 100 of the vessels, but by Navy request this was soon raised to 200. Contracts were given to the Consolidated Steel Corporation at Wilmington, Cal; to shipyards on the Great Lakes; to the two Kaiser yards of Richmond No 4 and at Vancouver, Wash, and later to the Jones-Brunswick and Southeastern SB yards. A number of these shipyards were already participating in the programme for corvettes (later classed as frigates) and some were ordered to change to the new type. The Kaiser Vancouver contract awarded in February 1944 was for a block of 60 vessels, but this was cancelled in favour of the yard building C4 ships. The Lakes-built ships had to go to sea via the Mississippi, being fitted out and commissioned at New Orleans.

Sixty-five of the vessels rushed through for completion in 1944/45 were to become the U.S. Navy's ALAMOSA class of cargo ship (pennant Nos AK 156-220) and were given County names. However, ten of them were incomplete at the end of the war and were not acquired, these being AK's 176-177, 196, 203-204 and 216-220.

GRAINGER, as a U.S. Navy cargo ship, on trials *The Log*

In all ten shipyards became involved in the building of this type. A total of 336 were authorised, but only 239 were finally delivered, these consisting of 208 of the AV1 type for the Commission, eight completed privately after the war — these being five for France (as AV8's) by Tampa SB Co and three for Chile by Welding Shipyards — another of the AV8 type fitted with a controllable pitch propeller and completed for the Commission as was one (designated AV6) with diesel electric propulsion. In addition 17 became refrigerated vessels of the R1-M-AV3 type and four others, also completed privately after the war were designated as twin screw lumber carriers of the C1-MT-BU1 type.

Most of the C1-M vessels were given names of nautical expressions — Knot, Bend, Splice, Eye etc, whilst others were given the prefix of Coastal. . . . . .

Of the considerable number which had already been built by mid-1945, some 30 or so were intended for operation under the British flag, being temporarily transferred on bareboat charter to the Ministry of War Transport. All were to be given 'Hickory' as the prefix to their name. By the July ten were completed with this prefix by the California yard of the Consolidated Steel Co (yard Nos 1316-1319 and 1321-1326) and under the British flag were sent East for service in the Pacific. At first they were operated by three British commercial companies, Indo-China SN Co (3 ships), China Nav. Co (5 ships) and Common Bros (2 ships). Later their operators changed somewhat and by 1947 when the vessels were technically all redelivered to the USMC they were operated by Mollers Ltd (3 ships), Common Bros (5 ships) and Andrew Weir & Co (2 ships).

Twelve vessels, also from Consolidated (yard Nos 1327-1338) were all intended for delivery with 'Hickory' names, but the end of the war brought an end to further transfers and the vessels were completed during September/October 1945 with Maritime Commission names prefixed by Coastal. . . . However, at the cessation of hostilities certain further 'Hickory' names had already been allocated for future acquisitions, being:

HICKORY CLIFF	HICKORY GROVE	HICKORY PEAK
HICKORY COPSE	HICKORY LAKE (II)	HICKORY SKAW
HICKORY CRAG	HICKORY MERE	HICKORY WEIR

In fact these names were not taken up although they are listed in some postwar shipping registers and it is likely that they were intended for the last six vessels (following 22 Hickories) from Consolidated shipyard's 55-ship programme (yard Nos 1339-1344) and the last three vessels from the Jones Construction Co's programme (yard Nos 201-203) — all of which were completed with the 'Coastal' prefix but without firm evidence of earlier allocated names, as all other 'Coastal's' had.

Postwar conversions of C1-M type vessels were many and varied, to barges, power plants, dredging facilities, fish processing plants, LNG carriers and to drilling ships, to name but a few. The latter, generally, were lengthened and the beam increased and often fitted with a high derrick but remained self-propelled, this including the first British drilling ship.

Converting vessels to drilling ships is complex but nevertheless works out very much cheaper than building a new vessel. Virtually only the hull is retained and this is substantially modified to accept the drilling rig and its associated equipment. With delivery dates of new vessels to be considered and the one-time pressing need for rigs the attractions of conversion were appreciated by more and more drilling companies, providing that they could locate a suitable hull.

The basic type of C1-M ship was a single screw, diesel driven vessel with raised poop and fo'c's'le decks, two complete decks, raked stem and cruiser stern and with machinery aft. There were three holds and a cargo/deep tank forward and a refrigerated cargo hold aft. Subdivided by six bulkheads these were carried watertight to the main deck and one bulkhead carried oil tight to the second deck. There was no sheer amidships but forward and aft there was a straight-line sheer on all decks. Masts were installed between Nos 1 and 2 and between Nos 2 and 3 hatches, with two kingposts at the after end of No 3 hatch. The masts were fitted with booms on both sides whilst the kingposts were so equipped only on the forward side.

All accommodation, offices and workshops except the carpenters shop were located aft, there being workshops and store spaces on the second deck. The crew quarters, galley, messroom and hospital were on the main deck; officer's quarters, messroom and generator room on the poop deck; Captain's quarters, radio and gyro rooms on the superstructure deck and the wheelhouse and chartroom above this on the bridge deck. The carpenters shop as well as the paint, oil, lamp and canvas rooms and the boatswain's stores were located in the fo'c's'le. The main machinery, weighing some 130 tons, was diesel of 1,750 bhp and turned a 3-bladed 11ft diam. propeller, to which it was connected by four lengths of shafting.

Details

Tonnages 3,805 gross
2,123 nett
7,435 displacement
5,032 deadweight
Cruising range 14,500 miles
Speed 11 knots
Crew 35

Measurements: 338 ft 6 in length oa
320 ft bp
50 ft breadth moulded
29 ft depth moulded
18 ft draught

C1-M-AV1 type

Built by Barnes-Duluth SB Co, Duluth, Minnesota (later Walter Butler Shipbuilders, Duluth yard).

MC Hull Nos 2175-2186	Yard Nos 53-64 (cancelled)
2239-2250	28-39 (transferred to Walter Butler Shipbuilders, Duluth, when the yard changed hands, becoming yard Nos 328-339).

Built by Walter Butler Shipbuilders, Duluth, Minn

MC Hull Nos 2239-2250	Yard Nos 328-339	
2137-2140	340-343	Transferred from Walter Butler, Superior yard.
2135-2136	344-345	

328 Laid down as CAPE SOMERSET 9.44 Completed as JAMES W. REESE. 1945: CRINGLE REEFER. 1950: To Marad Reserve, Suisun Bay. 4.1974: Scrapped Kaohsiung.

329 Laid down as CAPE STANHOPE 10.44 Completed as RODGER W. YOUNG. 1945: BOWLINE REEFER. 1950: To Marad Reserve, Suisun Bay. 7.1973: Scrapped Pusan.

330 Launched as ELMER J. BURR 10.44 Completed as CROWN REEFER. 27.1.1946: Grounded in heavy weather on Kirilof Point, Amchitka Island (voyage Dutch Harbor/Aleutians — army stores). Later refloated and towed to Kiska, Alaska, but declared a CTL. Offered for sale for scrapping.

331 WILLIAM G. FOURNIER 11.44 1944: STAR REEFER. 1950: To Marad Reserve, Suisun Bay. 7.1974: Offered for sale.

332 KENNETH E. GRUENNERT 12.44 1945: GROMMET REEFER. 1950: To USN as a storeship (T-AF 53).

On 13 December 1952 this vessel anchored off the port of Leghorn, Italy, with a cargo of Christmas fare for the American forces in Italy and Austria. In a heavy gale she dragged her anchors, grounded on rocks and broke in two. Early in 1953 her bow was salved and taken in to port. Later the stern followed and finally the wreck was sold for scrapping.

WILLIAM N. NELSON, completed as CABLE EYE *World Ship Photo Library*

333 LEWIS HALL 11.44 1945: MESH KNOT. 1948: UNION POWER. 1966: SEVEN STARS. 1967: TIMBER THREE. 10.1968: Scrapped Valencia.

334 Launched as JOE P. MARTINEZ 2.45 Completed as ROUND SPLICE. Served as Spare Parts ship (US Army). 1947: PVT JOSE F. VALDEZ (US Army). 1950: To USN as a coastal transport (APC 119) (same name). 1959: (Marad). 1961: Reacquired by USN, classed as a Special Mission ship (T-AG 169) and equipped to collect oceanographic, associated electro-magnetic radiation information and meteorological observations in support of marine environment programmes. Operated by MSTS for Naval Communications Command, with a civilian crew of 163 persons. 1970: To Marad Reserve, James River.

335 Launched as WILLIAM N. NELSON 7.45 12.3.1945: Hull transferred to Pendleton Shipyards, New Orleans, for completion. 25.3.1945: Transferred again, to Port Houston Iron Works, Houston, Texas, and completed as CABLE EYE. 1948: UNION STAR. 6.1968: Scrapped Kaohsiung.

336 Launched as ALEXANDER R. NININGER, JR. 3.45 Completed as ACORN KNOT. 1949: SGT GEORGE D. KEATHLEY (US Army). 1950: To USN as a coastal transport (T-APC 117) (same name). 1957: (Marad). 12.1966: Reacquired by USN and refitted for oceanographic work (T-AGS 35). Later stricken. 3.1972: Transferred to Taiwan Navy, renamed CHU HWA.

337 Launched as FRANK J. PETRARCA 3.45 Completed as ROBAND HITCH. 1946: JUTAHY. 1954: SARGENT. 1962: PAMIT. 1966: BAMBERO. 2.1970: Scrapped Castellon.

338 Launched as HAROLD W. ROBERTS 4.45 Completed as IRISH SPLICE. 10.1970: Scrapped Bilbao.

339 HONDA KNOT 4.45 Later to Marad Reserve. 11.1972: Scrapped Taipei. Note: This vessel and its C1-M sistership JUMPER HITCH were among the last ships to leave the Olympia, Wash. Reserve fleet anchorage before it was closed down. The anchorage had been in use for over 30 years and at one time had over 200 ships in it.

340 SHAMROCK KNOT 5.45 1947: MANAQUI. 1965: VICTORIA T. 1969: Sold in USA for conversion to a dredger, but deal not completed. 1971: Sold to Tampa SR & DD Co (for resale) renamed VAQULINE PIERCE. 1973: SANTIAGO EXPRESS. 1976: PAOLA IX.

SHAMROCK KNOT as MANAQUI *Vic Young*

341 FIADOR KNOT 5.45 1946: Sold commercial (same name). 1956: PETROCHEM. 5.1957: Converted to chemical carrier by Bethlehem Steel Co, Brooklyn. Fitted with vertical cylindrical pressure cargo tanks, (4,120 grt). 27.9.1970: Transferred to US Government, loaded with obsolete ammunition, towed to sea and scuttled off Delaware Bay in position 38.39N 72.41W.

342 LEVER'S BEND 6.45 1946: Sold commercial (same name). 1955: GALENA. 1967: Returned to Marad under Ship Exchange programme, laid up in Reserve, Olympia, Wash. 7.1972: Scrapped Taipei.

343 MANROPE KNOT 7.45 Later to Marad Reserve, Mobile, Ala. 8.1972: Sold for non-transportation use and moored at Chickasaw, Alabama.

MARLINE HITCH as the gas tanker METHANE PIONEER *Author's collection*

344 MARLINE HITCH 7.45

This vessel, like so many of its contemporaries, was completed too late for war service, making her first voyage in Nov. 1945. The following year she was sold to Panama owners, becoming DON AURELIO. Five years later she came under the ownership of the North Atlantic & Gulf SS Co and was renamed NORMARTI. In 1958 she was acquired to perform a major role, becoming jointly owned by the British Gas Council and Constock International Methane Ltd; to be converted to the world's first liquefied gas carrier and to transport an experimental cargo of liquid methane gas across the Atlantic.

Constock, an American company formed jointly by Continental Oil Co and the Union Stock Yard & Transit Co, had carried out research and development since 1951 into the project of carrying methane by sea. This had already been attained in the USA with barges but the conversion of this ship represented the first attempt to transport gas across the high seas.

To enable it to be transported the gas had to be liquefied and frozen and this required specially insulated storage.

The ship was converted to a gas tanker, and deepened by 12 ft, at the Mobile shipyard of the Alabama DD & SB Co, being equipped with five special tanks. These were made of aluminium with an insulation of balsa wood and an outer jacket of steel. Owned under the British flag by the newly-formed British Methane Ltd the vessel — renamed METHANE PIONEER and of 5,058 grt — was operated for them by Stephenson Clarke Ltd. After successful trials at Lake Charles and in the Gulf of Mexico, which lasted some three months, the vessel loaded 2,000 tons of liquid natural gas (LNG) and sailed for the UK on January 31, 1959, arriving on February 20. Carried at a temperature of minus 258° F, liquifaction of the gas reduced its volume to 1/600th of the space it occupied in gaseous form. In its original state the natural gas was estimated to have an equivalent of 530 therms per ton. Allowing for losses during conversion its nett value became some 480 therms, and thus this trial shipment was the equivalent to slightly under one million therms.

For discharge the LNG was pumped ashore by specially designed ships pumps with a 6 inch insulation. The storage tanks were themselves heavily insulated, but a continuous boil-off of gaseous methane from the liquid was contained and later pumped into the pipeline. The liquid methane was vaporised by heat exchange with water or steam, being reconverted to gas under pressure, this being used to convey the gaseous methane into the transmission lines for delivery to the normal gas system.

METHANE PIONEER, a stern view *John G. Callis*

In March 1960 the METHANE PIONEER, converted to test LNG transportation by sea, successfully proved the concept when it completed the last of seven trial transatlantic voyages from Lake Charles to Canvey Island, Essex. During these seven trips over 12,000 tons of methane were delivered and the runs provided valuable information when planning future large-ship operations. The success of the experiments was soon proven when vessels of over 20,000 gross tons were specially built as methane carriers, using the same UK terminal although carrying LNG from Algeria.

The METHANE PIONEER was subsequently sold, passing to Panama flag operators in 1967 and becoming ARISTOTLE. Later she became a storage vessel for use at Recife.

345 MAINSHEET EYE 8.45 1947: REPUBLICA DE COLOMBIA. 1964: CIUDAD DE TURBO.

MAINSHEET EYE as REPUBLICA DE COLOMBIA *World Ship Photo Library*

Built by Walter Butler Shipbuilders, Superior, Wis.

MC Hull Nos 2113-2134 Yard Nos 31-52
2135-2140 53-58(transferred to Walter Butler, Duluth, becoming yard Nos 340-345).

31 GADSDEN 9.44 Completed for the US Navy as a cargo ship (AK 182). 1946: (USMC). 1947: Sold commercial (same name). 1955: YOSU.

GLACIER as HYDRA, in 1956 *John G. Callis*

32 GLACIER (II) 10.44 Completed for the US Navy as a cargo ship (AK 183). 1946: (USMC). 1947: HYDRA. 1962: ASMA B. 7.1970: Scrapped Hsinkang, China.

33 GRAINGER 9.44 Completed for the US Navy as a cargo ship (AK 184). 1946: (USMC). 1947: reacquired by USN. 4.1960: Stricken, sold to California shipbreakers for scrapping.

34 GWINNETT 11.44 Completed for the US Navy as a cargo ship (AK 185). 1945: Reclassified as AG 92 and adapted to carry aviation supplies and spare parts, again reclassed, as AVS 5. 1946: (USMC). 1947: STE. HELENE. 1968: PRINCE K.L.

On October 11, 1968 the PRINCE K.L., on a voyage from Davao to Tandjong Mani, grounded off Bancoran Island in the Sulu Sea. Early salvage attempts proved abortive but the ship finally refloated on November 21 and was towed to Bolabac. Survey showed severe bottom damage: she was towed to Kota Kinabalu and subsequently arrested pending settlement between owners and salvors. The matter settled, she underwent temporary repairs and then sailed for Hong Kong and Manila. Full repairs proved uneconomic and in February 1970 she returned to Hong Kong for scrapping.

35 HABERSHAM 11.44 Completed for the US Navy as a cargo ship (AK 186). 1946: (USMC). 1947: ROSA THORDEN. 1952: PUSAN. 1977: SAM DAE.

36 HENNEPIN 12.44 Completed for the US Navy as a cargo ship (AK 187). 1950: reclassed as T-AK 187. 6.1960: Stricken, and 10.1960: scrapped Japan.

37 HERKIMER 12.44 Completed for the US Navy as a cargo ship (AK 188). 1950: reclassed as T-AK 188. 6.1973: Stricken. Later chartered to US Trust Territory Government of the Pacific Islands.

38 HIDALGO 3.45 Completed for the US Navy as a cargo ship (AK 189). 1946: (USMC). 1947: RIZE.

KENOSHA as RIO DALE *World Ship Photo Library*

39 KENOSHA 2.45 Completed for the US Navy as a cargo ship (AK 190). 1946: (USMC). 1947: RIO DALE. 1958: TORIAN. 1963: LARS VIKING. 1965: NEPTUNE V. 1967: ARABDRILL 2. (drilling tender).

This vessel was acquired by the Arabian Drilling Co, Saudi Arabia, and converted to an offshore drilling rig with fixed platform by Soc. Prov. Ateliers Terrin & Union Ind. d'Entreprise, Marseilles. She is fitted with a platform measuring 80 ft x 60 ft and a derrick 140 ft in height, has seven 11,000 lb anchors and is equipped for drilling — in the Persian Gulf — to a depth of 200 ft.

40 LEBANON 8.45 Completed for the US Navy as a cargo ship (AK 191). 1946: (USMC). 1946: COASTAL ARCHER. 1956: RIO PARAGUACU. 1976: IRAZU.

41 LEHIGH (II) 3.45 Completed for the US Navy as a cargo ship (AK 192). 1945: (USMC). 1946: COASTAL EXPOUNDER. 1947: RIO SOLIMOES. 1969: Scrapped Rio de Janeiro.

42 LANCASTER 4.45 Completed for the US Navy as a cargo ship (AK193). 1945: (USMC) renamed COASTAL RINGLEADER. 1956: RIO PIANCO.

MARENGO as the drilling ship CYCLONE *Lloyd's of London*

43 MARENGO 4.45 Completed for the US Navy as a cargo ship (AK 194). 1945: (USMC) renamed COASTAL SPARTAN. 8.1966: Main propelling machinery removed, converted by Boston Metals Co, Baltimore, to a dredging facility. 1972: Converted by Bethlehem Steel Co, to a drilling ship for Storm Drilling Co, Houston, Texas. Renamed CYCLONE. The conversion of this vessel was similar to that carried out on the same owners' other drilling ships, the HURRICANE (ex C1-M TAG KNOT) and TYPHOON (ex R1-M KARIN). 1975: OCEAN CYCLONE.

44 MIDLAND 4.45 Completed for the US Navy as a cargo ship (AK 195). 1945: (USMC) renamed COASTAL HARBINGER. 1948: UNION BANKER. 5.1970: Scrapped Kaohsiung.

45 Launched as MINIDOKA 5.45 Intended to be cargo ship (AK 196) for US Navy, but not acquired. Completed as COASTAL HERALD. 1956: RIO MIRANDA. 1974: MIROSAL. 5.1977: Scrapped Brazil.

PHOEBE KNOT as CHOLOMA *Eric Johnson*

46 PHOEBE KNOT 5.45 1947: CHOLOMA. 1966: AGUASCALIENTES. 1977: ANDELE.

47 CHAIN AND CROWN 6.45 1947: RIO GURUPI. 1969: Scrapped Rio de Janeiro.

48 CINCH KNOT 5.45 1947: Sold commercial (same name). 1949: ANN MARIE. 1955: MOKPO HO. 1958: MOKPO.

49 HAWSER EYE 6.45 1956: RIO PAQUEQUER. 1973: MARILU. 1973: MIROLESTE.

50 DRAGON FLY 7.45 1947: RIO AMAZONAS. 10.1969: Scrapped Rio de Janeiro.

51 SAMPAN HITCH 8.45 1963: Acquired by US Air Force, converted to Atlantic Missile Range ship, renamed E-45-1861 SAMPAN HITCH. 7.1964: Acquired by USN and operated by MSTS as T-AGM 18 (same name). 6.1968: Stricken to Marad Reserve, Suisun Bay. 4.1973: Scrapped Kaohsiung.

52 JACOB'S LADDER 8.45 1947: REPUBLICA DEL ECUADOR. 1964: CIUDAD DE MANTA. 1965: LSCO PLATYPUS.

Built by Consolidated Steel Co, Wilmington, Cal.

MC Hull Nos	2314-2331	Yard Nos	1219-1236
	2461-2473		1307-1319
	2563-2586		1321-1344
	2587-2588		1345-1346 (cancelled 14.8.45)

Sideways launch of DIAMOND KNOT in 1944 *The Log*

1219 DIAMOND KNOT 12.44

The DIAMOND KNOT and the steamer FENN VICTORY were in collision in fog on August 13, 1947 when off Race Rocks, Juan de Fuca Strait, British Columbia, whilst the former vessel was bound from Alaska to Seattle with a cargo of salmon. Assistance was called for, as the steamer kept the DIAMOND KNOT afloat with her cross-trees hooked over the other's bow. But the C1-M was badly holed and flooded and as the ships were pulled apart and taken in tow she sank in 125 ft of water. The ship was a total loss, but her valuable cargo — worth six times more than the ship itself — was salved by divers who cut away the port side of the vessel. Most of the tinned cargo was recovered undamaged in less than two months.

1220 TIMBER HITCH 1.45 1963: Acquired by US Air Force, converted to Atlantic Missile Range ship, renamed E-45-1848 TIMBER HITCH. 7.1964: Acquired by USN and operated by MSTS as T-AGM 17 (same name). 5.1968: Stricken to Marad Reserve, James River.

1221 CLOVE HITCH 1.45 9.1972: Scrapped Kaohsiung.

1222 TURK'S HEAD 2.45 1947: Transferred to Philippine flag (same name) and operated by USMC. 1957: PABLO. 3.1968: Scrapped Osaka.

1223 STAR KNOT 2.45 1948: MINDANAO. 16.1.1967: Struck rocks and grounded on Tablas Island, 12.37N 122.40E. 23.1.1967: Refloated, towed Romblon Island, thence Manila. Repairs uneconomic. 9.1968: Scrapped Formosa.

1224 LANYARD KNOT 2.45 1947: RIO TOCANTINS. 1971: Scrapped Rio de Janeiro.

1225 JUMPER HITCH 3.45 10.1972: Scrapped Taipei.

1226 SQUARE KNOT 3.45 1956: TANANA. 12.1970: Scrapped Portland, Ore.

1227 SNUG HITCH 3.45 1947: Transferred to Philippine flag (same name) and operated by USMC. 1957: SAMAR.

MAIDEN'S EYE as the heavy-lift ship COL. WILLIAM J. O'BRIEN *Skyfotos*

1228 MAIDEN'S EYE 4.45 1947: COL. WILLIAM J. O'BRIEN (US Army). 1950: Acquired by USN (AK 246) (same name). 1954: Converted by Todd Shipyard, Brooklyn, to a heavy lift ship with two 80-ton capacity cranes, redesignated (T-AK 246). 9.1973: Stricken, sold for scrapping in Spain.

1229 SAILOR'S SPLICE 4.45 12.1972: Scrapped Kaohsiung.

1230 HALF HITCH 5.45 1948: BAHIA DE MARIEL.

1231 SPAR HITCH 5.45 1948: COPAN. 1966: TLAXCALA. 19.12.1975: Sank in a storm 30m off Vera Cruz, Gulf of Mexico.

1232 BOWLINE KNOT 7.45 1947: Transferrred to Philippine flag (same name) and operated by USMC. 2.1971: Scrapped Portland Ore.

1233 CAT'S PAW 7.45 1947: RIO SAO FRANCISCO. 3.1970: Scrapped Rio de Janeiro.

1234 LONG SPLICE 9.45 1947: PVT. FRANK J. PETRARCA (US Army). 1950: Transferred to USN (AK 250) (same name). 4.1959: Stricken, but 7.1960: Reinstated in USN (T-AK 250). 10.1973: Stricken to Reserve.

1235 CROSSING HITCH 9.45 1948: CIUDAD DE BOGOTA 1964: SINU. 1966: GALVESTON NAVIGATOR. 1967: MAJURO. 1971: Scrapped Singapore.

1236 CROWN KNOT 10.45 1947: HUALLAGA. 1969: PAN DE AZUCAR. 1.1974: Seized at Guayaquil by Ecuadorean authorities pending settlement of a law suit. 9.3.1974: Caught fire in engine room. Beached by port authority to avoid sinking. Heavily fire damaged. Listed to port and later sank, with only masts and bridge top above water. CTL.

1307 SHEEPSHANK 5.45 1947: RIO GUAIBA.

This vessel grounded near Belem on 10 June 1961, and hogged. Efforts were made to stiffen the ship, but the light-weight materials carried away as the ship 'worked' on the high tides. On 27 June she broke in two and both parts floated. Attempts to bring the stern into the channel by utilising the ship's engines partly succeeded when it cleared the bow — only to ground again half a mile away. In mid-July this section again refloated and was towed to Belem, but by this time the bow had settled deeply into the sand. The ship was a total loss.

1308 BOATSWAIN'S HITCH 5.45 1947: Transferred to Philippine flag (same name) and operated by USMC. 1957: LUIS. 1971: LUISEVERETT. 9.1971: Scrapped Kaohsiung.

1309 REEF KNOT 5.45 1974: PACIFIC SHRIMPER (fish factory). 1978: ROYAL VENTURE.

1310 SHORT SPLICE 5.45 1950: Transferred to USN as AK 249 (same name). 1954: Converted by Todd Shipyard, Brooklyn, to a heavy lift ship with two 80-ton capacity cranes. Redesignated T-AK 249. 6.1973: Stricken in the Far East following the run-down of Military Sealift requirements after the ceasefire and withdrawal from Vietnam. 10.1973: Scrapped Hong Kong.

1311 MASTHEAD KNOT 5.45 1945: Transferred to Philippine flag (same name) and operated by USMC. 1957: MACTAN. 1966: GENERAL DEL PILAR. 13.5.1969: Caught fire after generator exploded in engine room whilst loading logs at Surigao, Mindanao. Entire ship engulfed and gutted. 16.5.1969: Sank in anchorage at General Island. CTL.

SWORD KNOT as a Range Instrumentation ship *U.S.N.*

1312 SWORD KNOT 5.45 1963: Acquired by US Air Force, converted to Range Instrumentation ship, renamed E-45-1852 SWORD KNOT. 7.1964: Acquired by USN and operated by MSTS for Air Force Space and Missile Test Centre, Vandenberg Air Base, Calif. at Western Test Range in Pacific. Pennant T-AGM 13. Civilian manned with crew of 12 officers, 30 men and 28 technicians. 4.1971: Stricken to Marad Reserve, Suisun Bay. 5.1973: Sold to California shipbreakers for scrapping.

1313 ANCHOR HITCH 6.45 11.1972: Scrapped Kaohsiung.

1314 HOOK HITCH 6.45 1947: RIO JURUA. 1948: ITAPEVA. 1952: RIO JURUA. 1969: Scrapped Rio de Janeiro.

1315 FISHERMAN'S BEND 6.45 1947: NAPO. 27.6.1965: Sprang leak, put aground on rocky beach 70 miles south of Coquimbo, Chile. Buckled and fractured, holds and engine room flooded. Abandoned in heavy seas. CTL. (Voyage Coquimbo/Valparaiso — sugar).

1316 HICKORY KNOLL 6.45 Chartered to British MOWT. 1947: (USMC). Operated by US Army. Later renamed WILLIAM J. SUTTON.

1317 HICKORY GHYLL 6.45 Chartered to British MOWT. 1947: (USMC). 1948: UNION CARRIER. 1966: TIMBER TWO. 5.1968: Scrapped Alicante.

1318 HICKORY BROOK 6.45 Chartered to British MOWT. 1947: (USMC), renamed MARLINE BEND. 8.1970: Scrapped Bilbao.

1319 HICKORY CREST 6.45 Chartered to British MOWT. 1947: (USMC). 1948: UNION MARINER. 17.4.1963: Grounded at Cayos Arios, ENE of Vera Cruz (voyage Tampa/Vera Cruz). 24.4.1963: Refloated, found not worthy of repair, sold for scrap. Resold and repaired, renamed TABASCO. 8.1974: Scrapped Bilbao.

1321 HICKORY GLEN 7.45 Chartered to British MOWT. 1947: SHERIDAN. 1960: MATUPI. 1964: TONG LAM. 22.10.1970: Grounded on Scarborough Reef, China Sea, 420 miles N.W. of Manila. Abandoned. Struck by typhoon, broke in three. Total loss. (Voyage N.Korea/Chittagong — pig iron).

1322 HICKORY MOUNT 7.45 Chartered to British MOWT. 1948: HEATHMORE. 1961: GRECIAN MED. 1969: IMATACA. 1.1972: Scrapped Bilbao.

1323 HICKORY ISLE 7.45 Chartered to British MOWT. 1947: BRESCIA. 1966: TIMBER ONE. 1970: Converted to oceanographic research ship and mining vessel, renamed DEEPSEA MINER. Used for the dredging and recovery of high-grade mineral nodules from the seabed. 1.1974: Scrapped Santander.

HICKORY STREAM, just transferred to the British flag as DOMINIC *World Ship Photo Library*

HICKORY STREAM as GOLDEN OCEAN, in the Malacca Straits *Airfoto, Malacca*

1324 HICKORY STREAM 7.45 Chartered to British MOWT. 1947: DOMINIC. 1962: SAMODRA MAS. 1964: LOMBARDUS. 1965: GOLDEN OCEAN. 2.6.1971: Sprang leak during storm off the Andaman Islands, Bay of Bengal. 3.6.1971: Sank 14.30N 87.30E (approx); (Voyage Hungnam/Visakhapatnam — magnesium clinker).

1325 HICKORY DALE 7.45 Chartered to British MOWT. 1947: (USMC), renamed PERSIAN KNOT. 1956: KUNSAN. 1961: DAEPORI.

As the KUNSAN this vessel was blown ashore in a strong gale and heavy swell at Mukho, South Korea, on December 26, 1958, whilst waiting at anchor, offshore and in an unprotected roadstead (along with N type steamer DOGYU, ex RODNEY BAXTER) to load coal dust in Mukho harbour. Salvage attempts included the fitting of jacks to both sides of the ship to help lift her in a similar heavy swell. Several refloating efforts were made and in March 1959 the tug reported failure of its final effort and that removal of salvage gear had commenced. The ship was declared a CTL. Two years later, in April 1961, the vessel was refloated by her original owners. Towed in, she was fully repaired and re-entered service as the DAEPORI.

1326 HICKORY BURN 7.45 Chartered to British MOWT. 1947: (USMC). 1948: UNION TRADER. 4.1971: Scrapped Kaohsiung.

1327 Launched as HICKORY BAY 9.45 Completed as COASTAL VIKING. 3.1970: Scrapped Panama City.

1328 Launched as HICKORY COLL 9.45 Completed as COASTAL DELEGATE. 1947: Sold commercial (same name). 9.1952: Converted by Bethlehem Steel Co, Hoboken, to a self-unloading bulk cement carrier (3,581 grt) for Great Lakes service. Renamed PAUL H. TOWNSEND. 4.1958: Lengthened by 108 ft by Great Lakes Eng. Works, Ashtabula, Ohio, (432 ft length oa, 4,302 grt).

HICKORY CAPE as the cargo barge/dredging facility COASTAL SCOUT *Vic Young*

1329 Launched as HICKORY CAPE 9.45 Completed as COASTAL SCOUT. 1966: Converted by Southern SB Co, Slidell, to a cargo barge and/or dredging facility. The conversion consisted primarily of removing the main machinery, auxiliary boiler, propeller and tail shaft and blanking off the stern tube. Cranes were fitted on deck. Name retained.

1330 Launched as HICKORY TOR 9.45 Completed as COASTAL SKIPPER. 1947: PETALI. 1961: ARIMATHEIAS. 1965: ARIMATHIAN. 1966: CARIBE. 10.10.1971: Reported by radio whilst on voyage from Barranquilla to Santo Domingo with cement clinker. Became overdue; no further trace, presumed sank.

1331 Launched as HICKORY BRAE 9.45 Completed as COASTAL ADVENTURER. 2.1971: Scrapped Seattle.

1332 Launched as HICKORY BOURNE 9.45 Completed as COASTAL NAVIGATOR. 1969: Converted by Levingston SB Co, Orange, Texas, to an offshore oil well drilling vessel (4,384 grt) and renamed NAVIGATOR.

1333 Launched as HICKORY DELL 9.45 Completed as COASTAL CHAMPION. 1947: Transferred to Philippine flag (same name) and operated by USMC. 1948: BRADEVERETT. 1962: PAULINO. 1970: Scrapped Hirao.

1334 Launched as HICKORY CAIRN 10.45 Completed as COASTAL CONQUEROR. 1956: RIO PIABANHA. 6.1970: Scrapped Rio de Janeiro.

1335 Launched as HICKORY DYKE 10.45 Completed as COASTAL RIDER. 1949: NORTH STAR (US Dept of the Interior, Bureau of Indian Affairs). 1963: PACIFIC ISLANDER (US Dept of the Interior, Trust Territory of the Pacific Islands). 6.1969: Scrapped Tadotsu, Japan.

1336 Launched as HICKORY TARN 10.45 Completed as COASTAL NOMAD. 9.1972: Scrapped Kaohsiung.

1337 Launched as HICKORY LAKE (I) 10.45 Completed as COASTAL BUCCANEER. 1948: REBEVERETT. 1962: GUILLERMO. 1968: Scrapped Onomichi.

1338 Launched as HICKORY BECK 11.45 Completed as COASTAL CADET. 1948: MAULE. 1961: CASTILLA. 7.6.1969: Parted moorings in a storm at San Antonio, Chile, and drifted on to rocks. Engine room and holds flooded. Divers later confirmed the feasibility of refloating, but repair costs were uneconomic and the vessel was adjudged to be a CTL.

1339 COASTAL RAMBLER 11.45 7.1972: Scrapped Kaohsiung.

1340 COASTAL MONARCH 12.45 7.1972: Scrapped Kaohsiung.

COASTAL CHARGER as BAHIA DE NIPE *Author's collection*

1341 COASTAL CHARGER 12.45 1948: BAHIA DE NIPE.

1342 COASTAL COURSER 11.45 1948: TROLLAFOSS. 1964: SEOUL. 29.8.1973: Dragged anchors in heavy weather at Inchon, S. Korea. Blown aground on to a concrete causeway where she became high and dry astride it, several feet above water level. Extensively damaged, back broken. Total loss. Sold and 2.1974: Scrapped in situ.

COASTAL COURSER as TROLLAFOSS *John G. Callis*

COASTAL MONITOR as EGYPTOS *Author's collection*

1343 COASTAL MONITOR 11.45 1947: KRIOS. 1961: EGYPTOS.

1344 COASTAL TELEGRAPHER 12.45 1948: PUNTA DEL ESTE. 8.1970: Sold to Uruguayan shipbreakers but resold for further trading (same name).

COASTAL TELEGRAPHER as PUNTA DEL ESTE *John G. Callis*

Built by Froemming Bros Inc, Milwaukee, Wis.

MC Hull Nos 2141-2150 Yard Nos 13-22
2350-2353 23-26

DUVAL as COASTAL RACER *World Ship Photo Library*

13 CHARLEVOIX 8.44 Completed for the US Navy as a cargo ship (AK 168). 1946: (USMC). 1947: BENNY. 1959: BENNY VIKING. 1963: BENNY. 1963: STELLA OCEANICA. 1965: JASOLINAN. 1966: PARASKEVI. 9.1970: Scrapped Castellon.

14 CHATHAM (II) 9.44 Completed for the US Navy as a cargo ship (AK 169). 1946: (USMC). 1947: HELENA. 1963: LINCOLN EXPRESS. 14.12.1972: Broke in two and 15.12.1972: sank during heavy weather west of San Juan P.R. in position 18.35N 66.29W (approx) (voyage Santo Domingo/Puerto Rico — gypsum rock).

15 CHICOT 10.44 Completed for the US Navy as a cargo ship (AK 170). 1946: (USMC). 1947: Transferred to USN. 1951: Transferred to US Department of the Interior. 1960: Sold commercial (same name). 1970: SAN LUIS. 4.1972: Sold to Hong Kong for scrapping but 1973: Converted to a lighter.

16 CLAIBORNE 11.44 Completed for the US Navy as a cargo ship (AK 171). 1946: (USMC). 1.1971: Sold; awaiting scrapping at Seattle.

17 CLARION 12.44 Completed for the US Navy as a cargo ship (AK 172). 1946: (USMC). 1947: LOVDAL. 1956: URUBAMBA. 1969: CEBU. 26.4.1970: Stranded in fog near Punta Negra, N. Peru. Pounded by heavy breakers, flooded and abandoned. Total loss. (Voyage Callao/Buenaventura — ballast).

18 CODINGTON 1.45 Completed for the US Navy as a cargo ship (AK 173). 1946: (USMC). 1956: POHANG. 11.11.1972: Damaged by mine explosion whilst discharging at Phnom-Penh, Khmer Republic. Proceeded to Saigon thence to Singapore for drydocking. Repairs uneconomic, laid up. Sold. 1.1974: Scrapped Kaohsiung.

19 COLQUITT 12.44 Completed for the US Navy as a cargo ship (AK 174). 1946: Acquired by US Coast Guard, based at Honolulu to perform logistic services in Pacific. Renamed KUKUI (WAK 186). 1953: Stricken from service.

20 CRAIGHEAD 4.45 Completed for the US Navy as a cargo ship (AK 175). 1946: (USMC). 1947: KASTAMONU.

21 Launched as DODDRIDGE 5.45 Intended to be cargo ship (AK 176) for US Navy, but not acquired. Completed as COASTAL MESSENGER. 1951: Acquired by US Coast Guard, renamed COURIER (WAGR 410).

Following her acquisition by the USCG the vessel was fitted out by Bethlehem Steel Co, Hoboken, as an overseas radio relay base, manned by the Coast Guard and operated for the US Information Agency as a relay station for the 'Voice of America' broadcasts from Sept. 1952 to May 1964. She was virtually a seagoing radio broadcasting station with transmitting equipment the most powerful of its kind ever installed in any vessel, and helped offset the effects of USSR jamming of US broadcasts.

Commissioned in February 1952, broadcasts began on September 7, the ship being stationed at the island of Rhodes, Greece. She returned to the USA in 1964 and decommissioned in the August. Recommissioned again on July 1, 1965, she was employed as a training cutter (WTR 410) for the USCG Reserve at Yorktown, Va. Her special equipment was removed and a helicopter platform added. Later she was again placed in Reserve in the James River.

22 Launched as DUVAL 6.45 Intended to be cargo ship (AK 177) for US Navy, but not acquired. Completed as COASTAL RACER. 1953: Acquired by USN. Converted by Gibbs Corpn, Jacksonville, Fla. to a floating electric power station, its steam operated power plant having a capacity of 34,500 Kw. Without means of propulsion the unit required to be towed wherever necessary. Designated YFP 10. 3.1975: Sold to Japanese buyers at Kobe.

23 KNOB KNOT 7.45 11.1971: Scrapped Brownsville, Texas.

24 SALMON KNOT 8.45 10.1970: Scrapped Bilbao.

25 YARD HITCH 9.45 1947: RIO MAGDALENA. 1966: DELTA. 1967: SAN BERNARDINO STRAIT. 8.12.1967: Sank near Aparri in position 19.40N 124.12E during a storm off Luzon (voyage Philippines/S. Korea — chemicals, ore and logs).

26 Launched as TAPIR SPLICE 10.45 Completed as BEN FROEMMING. 1947: RIO GUAYAS. 1966: GALVESTON LUMBERMAN. 1967: GOLDRILL 5. 1974: Converted to a drilling vessel.

TAPIR SPLICE as RIO GUAYAS *World Ship Photo Library*

Built by Globe Shipbuilding Co, Superior, Wis.

MC Hull Nos 2151-2158 Yard Nos 118-125
2505-2507 126-128(transferred from Leathem D. Smith, being their yard Nos 344-346)

118 MUSCATINE 11.44 Completed for the US Navy as a cargo ship (AK 197). 1946: (USMC). 1947: PALMA. 1953: AVANCE. 1968: DUKE K.L. 1972: Sold to Hong Kong shipbreakers but 1973: Cut down and converted to a lighter.

119 MUSKINGUM 10.44 Completed for the US Navy as a cargo ship (AK 198). Later reclassed T-AK 198. 6.1973: Stricken. Later chartered to U.S. Trust Territory Government of the Pacific Islands.

120 NICOLLET 11.44 Completed for the US Navy as a cargo ship (AK 199). 1945: Reclassed (AG 93) and then adapted to carry aviation supplies and spare parts, again reclassed (AVS 6). 1946: (USMC). 1948: DJERADA. 2.1970: Scrapped Valencia.

121 PEMBINA 11.44 Completed for the US Navy as a cargo ship (AK 200). 1951: reclassed T-AK 200. 1958: (Marad). 1968: RESOLUTE (US Army).

122 PEMISCOT 11.44 Completed for the US Navy as a cargo ship (AK 201). 1945: (USMC) renamed COASTAL COMPETITOR. 1956: RIO TUBARAO.

PINELLAS as BAHIA DE MATANZAS *Michael Lennon*

123 Launched as PINELLAS 3.45 Intended to be cargo ship (AK 202) for US Navy, but not acquired. Completed as COASTAL STEVEDORE. 1948: BAHIA DE MATANZAS. 1977: Reported sold for scrapping.

124 Launched as PIPESTONE 4.45 Intended to be cargo ship (AK 203) for US Navy, but not acquired. Completed as COASTAL EXPLORER. 1947: PUTUMAYO. 1968: FELIPE. 8.1974: Scrapped Bilbao.

125 Launched as PITKIN 5.45 Intended to be a cargo ship (AK 204) for US Navy, but not acquired. Completed as COASTAL OBSERVER. 1956: RIO MOCORO. 1971: GUARARAPES. 1974: SAO SEBASTIAO.

126 BIGHT KNOT 8.45 1947: CHOLUTECA. 1965: APOSTOLAKIS T. 1966: JEAN T. 1967: APOSTOLAKIS T. 1969: ESPERANZA. 8.7.1970: Stranded near Punta de Piedras, Margarita Island, Venezuela, due to the channel buoys being unlit. Refloating attempts made but vessel firmly embedded in sandy bottom. A channel was dug, the ship refloated and continued to destination for survey. However, she did not survive for long, being sold to shipbreakers and arriving as Split in April 1971.

127 OCEAN PLAT -.47 Launched in 1945: completed in 1947. 1947: RIO ORINOCO. 1960: DAISEI. 1962: DAISEI MARU. 9.1970: Reported scrapped Kainan, Japan.

128 MAGNUS HITCH 2.47 Launched in 1945; completed in 1947. 1947: REPUBLICA DE VENEZUELA. 1960: DAIKO. 1962: DAIKO MARU. 4.1971: Scrapped Ako, near Aioi, Japan.

Built by Kaiser Company Inc. Richmond Yard No 4, Richmond, Cal.

MC Hull Nos 2101-2112	Yard Nos 58-69
2374-2382	70-78
2509-2511	79-81

ALCONA as a U.S. Navy cargo ship, July 1946 *Charles N. Dragonette collection*

58 ALAMOSA 8.44 Completed for the US Navy as a cargo ship (AK 156). 1946: (USMC). 8.1972: Scrapped Portland, Ore.

59 ALCONA 9.44 Completed for the US Navy as a cargo ship (AK 157). 1955: To USN Reserve. 1960: Stricken, sold and scrapped.

60 AMADOR 10.44 Completed for the US Navy as a cargo ship (AK 158). 1946: (USMC). 1947: SKAGERN. 1963: NICOLAOS. 1972: DINA. 1973: ALKISTIS.

ANTRIM as KARS *A. Duncan*

61 ANTRIM 10.44 Completed for the US Navy as a cargo ship (AK 159). 1946: (USMC). 1947: KARS.

62 AUTAUGA 11.44 Completed for the US Navy as a cargo ship (AK 160). 1946: (USMC). 1947: HERSILIA. 1962: FAUZIA B. 1.1971: Scrapped Shanghai.

63 BEAVERHEAD 12.44 Completed for the US Navy as a cargo ship (AK 161). 1946: (USMC). 1947 HERA. 1963: OMAR EXPRESS. 5.1967: Converted by Avondale Shipyards, Avondale, La., to a self-unloading bulk cement carrier (3,617 grt) renamed CEMENTO PONCE. 1976: VANESSA.

64 BELTRAMI 12.44 Completed for the US Navy as a cargo ship (AK 162). 1955: To USN Reserve. 1960: Stricken, sold and scrapped.

BLOUNT as HECUBA. Note the extended bridge deck *Author's collection*

65 BLOUNT 1.45 Completed for the US Navy as a cargo ship (AK 163). 1946: (USMC). 1947: HECUBA. 1963: ANNA. 1965: PANOS. 1.1974: Scrapped Shanghai.

66 BREVARD 2.45 Completed for the US Navy as a cargo ship (AK 164). 1946: (USMC). 1947: ZEEHOND. 1948: HESTIA. 1962: LEILA B. 8.1970: Scrapped Tientsin, China.

67 BULLOCK 3.45 Completed for the US Navy as a cargo ship (AK 165). 1946: (USMC). 1947: EDIRNE. 1948: ADANA. 1948: MALATYA.

68 CABELL 4.45 Completed for the US Navy as a cargo ship (AK 166). 1946: (USMC). 1947: SOMMEN. 1963: DONALD. 10.1963: Posted missing after last reporting on 25 Aug. 1963 in Gulf of Aden when on voyage from Ploce to Djakarta with concrete reinforcing bars.

69 CALEDONIA 3.45 Completed for the US Navy as a cargo ship (AK 167). 1946: (USMC). 1947: NORSE CAPTAIN. 1962: MABINI. 1963: PRESIDENT QUEZON. 1965: SEVEN KINGS.

70 FAIRFIELD 3.45 Completed for the US Navy as a cargo ship (AK 178). 1946: (USMC). 1.1946: Reported transferred to the Japanese Government, at Yokosuka.

71 FARIBAULT 4.45 Completed for the US Navy as a cargo ship (AK 179). 1946: (USMC). 1947: Reacquired by USN. 1956: To USN Reserve. 1960: Stricken, scrapped Oakland, Cal.

72 FENTRESS 5.45 Completed for the US Navy as a cargo ship (AK 180). 1946: (USMC). 1950: re-acquired by USN, reclassed T-AK 180. 10.1973: Stricken. Later chartered to U.S. Trust Territory Government of the Pacific Islands.

73 FLAGLER 5.45 Completed for the US Navy as a cargo ship (AK 181). 9.10.1945: Grounded off Okinawa in typhoon. Refloated and 1946: Returned to USMC. 1948: Sold and 1949: Reported scrapped Shanghai.

74 SQUARE SINNET 5.45 1956: TATALINA. 1971: ATALINA. 1975: COLIMA.

75 GUNNER'S KNOT 6.45 1953: Transferred to US Dept of Interior, Trust Territory of the Pacific Islands. 12.1977: Scrapped Kaohsiung.

76 MOORING KNOT 6.45 1947: RIO IPIRANGA. 6.1970: Scrapped Rio de Janeiro.

77 SPINDLE EYE 6.45 Acquired by US Army as a news transmission ship. 1947: SGT CURTIS F. SHOUP (US Army). 1950: (Marad). 3.1963: Acquired by USN and classed as survey support ship (T-AG 175) (same name), being fitted for gravity and magnetic survey. Operated by MSTS for Naval Oceanographic Office by a civilian crew of 44 plus 42 technicians. 1.1970: To Marad Reserve, Suisun Bay. 9.1973: Scrapped Kaohsiung.

78 MARLINGSPIKE HITCH 8.45 1947: Transferred to Philippine flag (same name) and operated by USMC. Later to Marad Reserve, Suisun Bay. 4.1973: Scrapped Terminal Island, Cal.

79 TERMINAL KNOT 9.45 1949: SUSITNA. 6.1970: Scrapped Portland, Ore.

80 SPOOL SINNET 8.45 1947: RIO OIAPOQUE

An interesting casualty occurred to this ship on October 5, 1954 when she was in collision with her sistership RIO SOLIMOES (Walter Butler, yard No 41) off Itacoatiara, Brazil. The RIO OIAPOQUE was beached with a gaping 45 ft x 30 ft hole in her port side, with hatch coamings and bulkheads carried away. In Manaus her owners obtained steel plates, angle iron and rails and following the arrival of salvors on November 17 plate patches and timber/steel mattresses were fitted over the opening. Refloated on December 2 she was towed to Manaus and after further temporary repair proceeded to Mobile, Ala.

Strangely, this ship and the vessel she collided with in 1954 were jointly offered for sale in 1968 as 'unserviceable cargo vessels lying in Brazilian ports'. Linked with them and similarly described was another sistership, the RIO PARNAIBA.

The RIO OIAPOQUE was scrapped in Brazil in 1969.

81 REEVING EYE 9.45 1946: DON ANSELMO. 1951: NORPALMA. 1956: MANTARO. 1971: SOTIHUE. 1971: TOBAGO. 30.8.1971: Sunk in collision with Ecuadorean Navy escort patrol vessel MANABI near Cape San Lorenzo, Ecuador (voyage Callao/Buenaventura — ballast).

Built by Kaiser Company Inc., Vancouver, Washington.

MC Hull Nos 2254-2313 Yard Nos 501-560 (contract for 60 ships awarded in Feb. 1944 but cancelled to enable yard to build C4 type ships).

Built by J.A. Jones Construction Co. Brunswick, Ga.

MC Hull Nos	Yard Nos
2474-2484	190-200
2726-2728	201-203
2729-2739	204-214(cancelled)

190 LOCK KNOT 6.45 1947: PVT GEORGE J. PETERS (spare parts ship, US Army). 1950: To Marad Reserve, Suisun Bay. 10.1974: Reported sold to Panama buyers for conversion/further service, but currently still laid up at Suisun Bay.

191 RING SPLICE 6.45 2.1971: Scrapped Portland, Ore.

192 SINNET 7.45 7.1970: Scrapped Bordentown, NJ.

193 CROWN AND DIAMOND 7.45 4.1972: Scrapped Brownsville, Texas.

194 BELL RINGER 8.45 1947: CAPT ARLO L. OLSEN (US Army). 1950: Transferred to USN as cargo ship (AK 245) (same name). 1950: became T-AK 245. 1958: (Marad). 5.1971: Scrapped Portland, Ore.

RIGGER'S EYE as ANTEN, with rebuilt superstructure and lengthened bridge deck *Author's collection*

195 RIGGER'S EYE 8.45 1947: NORDANBRIS. 1948: NORMUNDO. 1951: ANTEN. 1963: STELIOS M. 5. 1978: Scrapped Karachi.

196 SPAN SPLICE 9.45 4.1972: Scrapped Brownsville, Texas.

197 TRUE KNOT 10.45 8.1970: Sold, used as a floating store at Jersey City, NJ.

198 SHELL BAR 9.45 6.1970: Sold, converted to a floating storage barge.

199 MOORING HITCH 10.45 8.1972: Sold, converted to a drilling rig by Todd Shipyards, Galveston. Renamed KATHLEEN M. 1976: CANMAR EXPLORER II.

200 TAG KNOT 9.45 8.1972: Sold to California shipbreakers for scrap. 9.1973: Scrapping order rescinded, permitting vessel to be used for non-transportation purposes. 1973: Converted by Bethlehem Steel Co, Beaumont, Texas, to a drilling vessel. Renamed HURRICANE. 1975: OCEAN HURRICANE.

This vessel is in the same class as the drilling ships TYPHOON (ex R1-M KARIN) and CYCLONE (ex C1-M MARENGO). This class of vessel has the capability of drilling in waters up to 600 ft deep. The conversion of the HURRICANE involved installation of a new midship section which increased the vessel's length to 380 ft from 338 ft. She was widened by the addition of 10 ft wide sponsons on either side for a length of 250 ft. This modification increased the beam to 70 ft. She was also fitted with two 50 ft Mariner cranes and a mooring system with four double-drum winches spooling 3,250 ft of $2\frac{3}{4}$ in. wire rope.

Resistance to wave motion is accomplished with a Flume system and two roll stabilisers each 145 ft x 4 ft. The HURRICANE differs from her predecessors in some respects. For example, the same power source that propels the ship is used for the drilling operation. The original single diesel propulsion engine has been replaced with electric motor drive, the central power system being three 1,500 Kw generators powered by diesels. D.C. power for propulsion and rig operation is converted through an SCR system.

201 COASTAL MARINER 10.45 1951: (To Reserve). 14.7.1965: Scuttled in the Atlantic off New Jersey coast with obsolete ammunition.

202 COASTAL CAPTAIN 10.45 1948: ANDINO. 1964: GERTRUD C. ERTEL. 1966: I.C. ERTEL. 1967: ROTTERDAM.

203 COASTAL RANGER 12.45 1948: UNION BUILDER. 9.1969: Scrapped Kaohsiung.

COASTAL RANGER as UNION BUILDER *Airfoto, Malacca*

Built by J.A. Jones Construction Co., Panama City.

MC Hull Nos 2748-2753 Yard Nos 109-114 (contracts transferred from Southeastern SB but subsequently cancelled 14.8.1945).

Built by Pennsylvania Shipyards Inc., Beaumont, Texas.

MC Hull Nos	2333-2337	Yard Nos	332-336
	2340-2349		339-348
	2620-2623		353-356
	2754-2758		365-369
	2760-2789		371-400 (cancelled, intended to become C1-M-AV8 type).

332 HAWSER BEND 4.45 1947: Transferred to Philippine flag (same name) and operated by USMC. 1948: LENEVERETT. 1962: LEONARD. 7.1970: Scrapped Hirao.

333 CARRICK BEND 4.45 1947: Transferred to Philippine flag (same name) and operated by USMC. 1957: Sold commercial (same name). 1960: SIQUIJOR.

The SIQUIJOR, bound from Japan to Iligan with a cargo of machinery, ran aground in poor visibility at Tagolo Point, 140 miles south east of Iloilo City in the Philippines on July 21, 1969 — at a time when the south west monsoon blows with unpredictable force in the area. Despite the ship making water through fractures in her hull in rising seas she was refloated four days later, and towed to Dapitan Bay. Later she was towed to Manila where heavy bottom damage was revealed. Repairs proved uneconomic and the ship was sold, being scrapped at Kaohsiung in December 1970.

ROSE KNOT as the U.S. Navy's Missile Range ship *Author's collection*

334 ROSE KNOT 5.45 1963: Acquired by US Air Force, converted to Atlantic Missile Range ship, renamed E-45-1850 ROSE KNOT. 7.1964: Acquired by USN and operated by MSTS as T-AGM 14 (same name). 3.1968: Stricken to Marad Reserve, Suisun Bay.

335 WALL KNOT 5.45 1947: NORVANA. 1959: LAGO VIKING. 1963: AN DONG.

336 SPANISH BOWLINE 5.45 1945: (Spare parts ship, US Army). 1947: HUBERT PROM. 1968: BARON K.L. 8.2.1971: Sank after collision with tanker METHONI (29,139 grt, 1958) 230 miles N.W. of Manila in position 17.47N 118.55E (voyage Hong Kong/Poro Point — ballast).

339 EMERALD KNOT 6.45 1956: RIO JAGUARIBE. 1976: CIUDAD DE ITAGUI.

340 CABLE SPLICE 7.45 1947: BANDEIRANTE. 1954: HOEGH ABEILLE. 1964: VELOX. 1966: NARWA. 1968: ELEFTHEROTRIA. 8.1970: Scrapped Perama.

341 BLACKWALL HITCH 7.45 1947: RIO PARNAIBA. 1969: Scrapped Rio de Janeiro.

RING KNOT as RIO DOCE *World Ship Photo Library*

342 RING KNOT 7.45 1947: RIO DOCE.

343 SHEET BEND 8.45 1947: NORINDIES. 1957: SAIGON MARU. 1966: EUN HA.

344 STUDDING SAIL 8.45 1947: Transferred to Philippine flag (same name) and operated by USMC. 1948: NOREVERETT. 1962: FERNANDO. 1968: Scrapped Shodoshima.

345 MARINER'S SPLICE 8.45 1946: MABAY. 1965: NICODEMOS. 30.9.1971: Grounded off Serrana Bank, Caribbean, in position 14.30N 80.20W. Salvage tug proceeded but after reporting holds of vessel open to the sea and cargo washing out departed from scene. Later information stated local parties were preparing to seize ship and remaining cargo, claiming that the ship had been abandoned. CTL. (Voyage Houston/Acajutla — sulphate and urea).

MARINER'S SPLICE as MABAY *Eric Johnson*

346 ANCHOR BEND 9.45 1956: RIO JEQUITINHONHA. 1970: Scrapped Rio de Janeiro.

347 BUNTLINE HITCH 9.45 1967: RELIANCE (US Army). Later to Marad Reserve, James River. 3. 1973: Sold to U.S. shipbreakers. 5. 1977: Scrapped Kearny NJ.

348 ROLLING HITCH 9.45 1946: BURSA. 1954: HOEGH ARONDE. 21.3.1963: Sprang leak in a gale, listed to 40 degrees and reported sinking in position 31.30N 10.35W, off Moroccan coast, (voyage Sassandra/Valencia — logs and phosphate). No further trace but logs from deck cargo found floating in sea.

353 CAPSTAN KNOT 10.45 1956: CHEJU.

354 HAWSER SPLICE 10.45 1956: RIO IGUACU. 1971: CIDADE DE ALCANTARA.

355 LOOP KNOT 10.45 1956: MUKHO. 9.1976: Scrapped Karachi.

356 RUNNING KNOT 11.45 1956: INCHON.

365 WATER KNOT 11.45 6.1972: Scrapped Brownsville, Texas.

366 TUCKED BEND 11.45 1956: RIO CAPIBARIBE.

367 THIMBLE EYE 11.45 1947: PACHITEA. 1965: GILDA JULIA. 1967: AMANDA. 10.1969: Scrapped Bilbao.

368 LEADER LOOP 11.45 1948: UNION PIONEER. 11.1970: Scrapped Kaohsiung.

369 BECKET HITCH 12.45 1956: CHANGHANG. 12.1975: Scrapped Busan.

Built by Leathem D. Smith Shipbuilding Co., Sturgeon Bay, Wis.

MC Hull Nos 2159-2174	Yard Nos 325-340
2505-2507	344-346 (transferred to Globe SB Co and completed as their yard Nos 126-128)
2508	347 (design changed to C1-ME-AV6 type)

325 POINSETT 9.44 Completed for the US Navy as a cargo ship (AK 205). 1946: (USMC). 1947: CARINA. 1953: MASAN.

POINSETT as a Navy cargo ship *U.S.M.C.*

326 PONTOTOC 10.44 Completed for the US Navy as a cargo ship (AK 206). 1945: Reclassified AG 94 and then Aviation Store ship AVS 7 (for carriage of aviation supplies and spare parts). 1946: (USMC). 1947: TAURUS. 1960: TADGERA. 1964: MYRIAM. 12.1968: Scrapped Valencia.

327 RICHLAND 11.44 Completed for the US Navy as a cargo ship (AK 207). 1946: (USMC). 1972: Sold to US buyers for conversion/scrapping.

328 ROCKDALE 11.44 Completed for the US Navy as a cargo ship (AK 208). 1946: (USMC). 1947: APOLLO. 1952: THABOR. 1960: ETIENNE DENIS. 1962: HONGKONG PIONEER. 9.7.1969: Struck Apo Reef, Mindoro Strait, Philippines, in a tropical storm. Sprang leaks, settled on bottom. 16.7.1969: Refloated, towed Manila. Temporarily repaired. A few local voyages made, and 5.1970: Scrapped Kaohsiung.

329 SCHUYLER 12.44 Completed for the US Navy as a cargo ship (AK 209). 1946: (USMC). 4.1971: Scrapped Tacoma, Wash.

SCREVEN as NORLINDO *World Ship Photo Library*

330 SCREVEN 1.45 Completed for the US Navy as a cargo ship (AK 210). 1946: (USMC). 1947: NORLINDO. 1959: Transferred to Peruvian Navy as a cargo ship, renamed ILO (pennant 133). 10.1968: Scrapped Valencia.

331 SEBASTIAN 1.45 Completed for the US Navy as a cargo ship (AK 211). 1945: To USMC, renamed COASTAL HIGHFLYER. 1967: RESOLVE (US Army).

332 SOMERSET 2.45 Completed for the US Navy as a cargo ship (AK 212). 1945: To USMC, renamed COASTAL SENTRY. 1947: To US Army, same name. 1950: (USMC). 1963: Acquired by US Air Force, converted to Missile Range ship, renamed E-45-1849 COASTAL SENTRY. 7.1964: Acquired by USN and operated by MSTS as T-AGM 15 (same name). 7.1968: Stricken, sold to shipbreakers.

This vessel and the steam tanker CERBERUS were lying 100 yards offshore at Hong Kong in September 1968 being broken up when a severe explosion occurred in a tank of the CERBERUS, still containing oil. Her tanks were blown out, shell plating blown open, the decks buckled and her bridge collapsed. The subsequent fire ignited drummed oil on deck and this in turn ignited the COASTAL SENTRY lying alongside — which herself still carried nearly 60,000 gallons of diesel oil aboard. The fire on this ship raged for some 15 hours before being extinguished, the vessel gutted in her engine room and accommodation and severely listing due to the quantity of water used for fire fighting.

Of prime concern to the shipbreakers was the quantity of steel no longer re-rollable and the loss of usable equipment.

333 SUSSEX 3.45 Completed for the US Navy as a cargo ship (AK 213). 1946: To Reserve. 1947: Re-acquired by USN. 1960: Stricken; sold to New York shipbreakers.

334 TARRANT 3.45 Completed for the US Navy as a cargo ship (AK 214). 1945: To USMC, renamed COASTAL ADVOCATE. 1947: RIO GUAPORE. 1948: ITAMAR. 1952: RIO GUAPORE. 1969: Scrapped Rio de Janeiro.

WEXFORD as the U.S. Navy's Missile Range ship COASTAL CRUSADER *Author's collection*

335 TIPTON 4.45 Completed for the US Navy as a cargo ship (AK 215). 1946: Transferred to US Coast Guard, renamed UNALGA (pennant WAK 185). 1951: To USMC, again renamed TIPTON. 7.1974: Converted to a fish cannery factory and anchored at Dutch Harbor, Alaska. Renamed SEA ALASKA. 1978: Reported to be broken up.

336 Launched as TRAVERSE 4.45 Intended to be cargo ship (AK 216) for US Navy, but not acquired. Completed as COASTAL MERCHANT. 1946: NORLANTIC. 1959: LEIF VIKING. 7.1.1962: Grounded in rough seas off Watch Hill Point, Rhode Island (voyage Searsport/New York — paper). 16.1.1962: refloated, towed Brooklyn. Declared a CTL and sold. 6.1962: Scrapped Rossville, Staten Island.

337 Launched as TULARE 5.45 Intended to be cargo ship (AK 217) for US Navy, but not acquired. Completed as COASTAL CHALLENGER. 1946: PACHITEA. 1954: DUNSTAN. 1958: SALLUST. 1959: MALACCA. 1963: TONG HONG. 20.12.1967: Posted missing after sailing from Kawasaki on 25 October 1967 bound for Colombo with a cargo of ammonium sulphate. No further trace, presumed sunk.

338 Launched as WASHTENAW 6.45 Intended to be cargo ship (AK 218) for US Navy, but not acquired. Completed as COASTAL GUIDE. 1947: SGT. GEORGE PETERSON (US Army). 1950: Transferred to USN (AK 248) (same name). 3.1959: Stricken to Marad Reserve. 12.1971: Sold, to be renamed MARSHA LYNN and anchored off Bayport, Gulf of Mexico, as a private fishing retreat.

339 Launched as WESTCHESTER 6.45 Intended to be cargo ship (AK 219) for US Navy, but not acquired. Completed as COASTAL DEFENDER. 1956: RIO MARACANA. 1969: Scrapped Rio de Janeiro.

340 Launched as WEXFORD 7.45 Intended to be a cargo ship (AK 220) for US Navy but not acquired. Completed as COASTAL CRUSADER. 1947: PVT JOE R. HASTINGS (US Army). 1950: (Marad). 1955; COASTAL CRUSADER. 1963: Acquired by US Air Force, converted to Missile Range ship, renamed E-45-1851 COASTAL CRUSADER. 7.1964: Acquired by USN and operated by MSTS as T-AGM 16 (same name) in support of Air Force Eastern test range in Atlantic. 12.1969: Reclassified as a survey ship (T-AGS 36) but taken out of service and placed in Suisun Bay Reserve fleet.

Built by Southeastern Shipbuilding Corp., Savannah, Ga.

MC Hull Nos	2485-2502	Yard Nos	AV 1-18
	2503-2504		AV19-20 (cancelled)
	2740-2747		AV21-28 (cancelled)
	2748-2753		AV29-34 (contract transferred to Jones, Panama, as their hull Nos 109-114, but later cancelled).

AV 1 CHECK KNOT 6.45 1947: SGT JOSEPH E. MULLER (US Army). 1950: Acquired by USN, operated by MSTS and designated as a coastal transport (T-APC 118) (same name). 1957: (Marad). 1962: Re-acquired by USN, classed as a Special Mission ship (T-AG 171) and equipped to collect oceanographic, associated electro-magnetic radiation information and meteorological observations in support of marine environment programmes. Operated for Naval Communications Command by a civilian crew of 169 persons. 12.1969: To Marad Reserve, James River. 9.1972: Sold for scrapping in USA.

AV 2 BECKET BEND 7.45 1947: PVT JOHN. F. THORSON (US Army). 1950: Acquired by USN (T-AK 247) (same name). 10.1958: Stricken. 1960: Sold for scrapping.

AV 3 FLEMISH KNOT 8.45 4.1971: Scrapped Portland, Ore.

AV 4 SNAKEHEAD 9.45 In Resrve, Mobile, Ala. 8.1972: Sold, converted by Todd Shipyards, Galveston, to a drilling rig. Renamed MARY J. 1976: CANMAR EXPLORER.

AV 5 LINK SPLICE 8.45 1947: SGT JONAH E. KELLEY (US Army). 1950: Acquired by USN, designated as a coastal transport (T-APC 116) (same name). 12.1969: To Marad Reserve, James River. 10.1972: Reported sold to New York shipbreakers.

AV 6 DIAMOND HITCH 10.45 In Reserve, Mobile, Ala. 8.1972: Sold, but laid up awaiting resale. 1975: Converted to a drilling ship by Avondale Shipyard, New Orleans. Renamed DELTA NINE.

PERSIAN KNOT as CANCHE *World Ship Photo Library*

AV 7 Launched as PERSIAN KNOT .47 Launched in 1945. Construction suspended, vessel turned over incomplete to USMC on 20.9.1945. Completed for French Government by Tampa SB Co as their hull No 158, (C1-M-AV8 type), renamed CANCHE. 1955: SUN GLEAM. 1963: STELLA ATLANTICA. 1965: ADRIATIC. 2.1969: Scrapped Spezia.

AV 8 Launched as MARLINE BEND .46 Launched in 1945. Construction suspended, vessel turned over incomplete to USMC on 20.9.1945. Completed for French Government by Tampa SB Co as their hull No 159 (C1-M-AV8 type), renamed BRESLE. 1964: MERRY MED. 1969: AROA. 1971: ARIMAR. 26.10.1971: Explosion in engine room, caught fire and grounded at Egg Island, off Eleuthera, in position 25.28N 76.54W, having left Nassau, Bahamas, the previous day after putting in for repairs. Abandoned. Total Loss. (Voyage Boca Grande/Venice — phosphate).

CROSSING KNOT as RADIANT MED *Michael Lennon*

AV 9 Launched as RING HITCH .47 Launched in 1945. Construction suspended, vessel turned over incomplete to USMC on 20.9.1945. Completed for Chilean owners by Welding Shipyards Inc, Norfolk, Va., renamed ANTARTICO.

AV 10 Launched as GRASS KNOT .48 Launched in 1945. Construction suspended, vessel turned over incomplete to USMC on 20.9.1945. Completed for Chilean owners by Welding Shipyards Inc, Norfolk, Va., renamed ALMAGRO. 1964: ADRIAN MARIS. 1965: ADRIAMARE. 1969: APOSTOLOS VENTOURIS. 1970: KIMOLOS B. 1974: SANTA MARIA B. 1975: SISKINA. 2.6.1976: Sank off Astipalaia Island, Aegean Sea, after striking rocks (voyage Braila/Saudi Arabia — cement).

AV 11 Launched as SAILMAKER'S SPLICE .48 Launched in 1945. Construction suspended, vessel turned over incomplete to USMC on 20.9.1945. Completed for Chilean owners by Welding Shipyards Inc, Norfolk, Va., renamed AMADEO. 1967: MAR CARIBE.

AV 12 LONG EYE 10.45 3.1967: Scrapped Panama City.

AV 13 Launched as CROSSING KNOT .46 Launched in 1945. Construction suspended, vessel turned over incomplete to USMC on 20.9.1945. Completed for French Government by Tampa SB Co as their hull No 160 (C1-M-AV8 type), renamed DIVES. 1964: RADIANT MED. 10.1972: Scrapped Perama.

SOLID SINNET as SERENE MED *Author's collection*

AV 14 Launched as SOLID SINNET .46 Launched in 1945. Construction suspended, vessel turned over incomplete to USMC on 20.9.1945. Completed for the French Government by Tampa SB Co as their hull No 161, (C1-M-AV8 type), renamed AULNE. 1965: SERENE MED. 1972: ATHEN.

AV 15 Launched as FLAT KNOT .46 Launched in 1945. Construction suspended, vessel turned over incomplete to USMC on 20.9.1945. Completed for the French Government by Tampa SB Co as their hull No 162, (C1-M-AV8 type), renamed COUESNON. 1963: EASTERN JUPITER. 1970: Scrapped Osaka.

AV 16 HORSESHOE SPLICE 10.45 In Reserve, Mobile, Ala. 1972: Sold, and 8.1974: Converted by Bethlehem Steel Co, Beaumont, Texas, to a drilling ship. Renamed TEMPEST. 1975: OCEAN TEMPEST.

AV 17 DOUBLE LOOP 10.45 1947: CIUDAD DE CARACAS. 1961: CYPROS.

AV 18 HALF KNOT 10.45 1948: BAHIA DE NUEVITAS. 12.1973: Scrapped Castellon.

DOUBLE LOOP as CIUDAD DE CARACAS *World Ship Photo Library*

C1-ME-AV6 type

The single vessel of this type was fitted with diesel electric propelling machinery of 2,200 hp.

Built by Leathem D. Smith Shipbuilding Co, Sturgeon Bay, Wis.

MC Hull No 2508 Yard No 347

347 COASTAL LIBERATOR 10.45 1948: CARRASCO. 10.1968: Used by Uruguayan Government as a convict ship 'temporarily lodging detainees'. 8.1970: Reported sold to Uruguayan shipbreakers, but resold for further trading, renamed PUNTA BEAGLE.

COASTAL LIBERATOR as CARRASCO, at New York *World Ship Photo Library*

C1-M-AV8 type

Only a single vessel of this type was originally completed, by the Bethlehem Steel Co, the ship being fitted with a controllable pitch propeller.

Later, five vessels of the C1-M-AV1 type, launched in 1945 by the Southeastern Shipbuilding Corpn (yard Nos AV 7/8 and AV 13/15) but then laid aside incomplete were acquired by the French Government. These were completed to the AV8 designation during 1946-47 by the Tampa SB Co.

Built by Pennsylvania Shipyards Inc., Beaumont, Texas (later Bethlehem Steel Co).

MC Hull No 2759 Yard No 370

SINGLE HITCH as the drillship DALMAHOY, in Australian waters *Christian Salvesen (Managers) Ltd*

370 SINGLE HITCH 12.45 To USMC Reserve. 12.1969: Sold to Houston buyers for non-transportation use. Resold to British buyers for conversion to a drilling ship.

Salvesen Offshore Drilling Ltd, a subsidiary of Christian Salvesen Ltd, Edinburgh, Scotland, became the first British company to break into the business of drillship contracting when they took delivery of a specially converted self-propelled drilling ship toward the end of 1973.

Purchased as the SINGLE HITCH, she was converted by the Tampa SB Co and renamed DALMAHOY. Her length was increased with a new 49 ft midbody to 389 ft and her beam by 28 ft to 78 ft. Towering above her maindeck is a 160 ft-high derrick, mounted on a 30 ft-high base. All this allows drilling in water up to 700 ft deep and through the earth's core to depths up to 20,000 ft.

Other equipment aboard includes a heli-landing deck, sub-sea television systems and a motion compensator which provides a stable working platform in all but exceptional weather conditions. The anchoring system includes eight 30,000 lwt anchors with four 20,000 lwt back-up anchors. The ship's diesel propulsion was replaced with electric motor drive.

The first British-owned drill ship, she has worked off Australia, and Indonesia, in the Indian Ocean and in the Red Sea under the Salvesen flag.

The Salvesen concern have operated ships in the traditional tramping trades since their formation in 1846. They have a major stake in servicing North Sea exploration and their interests also embrace shipping, cold storage fish processing and other non-marine operations. In January 1979 DALMAHOY was sold to Canadian Marine Drilling, delivered in Singapore and renamed CANMAR EXPLORER IV.

C1-MT-BU1 type

These vessels were twin screw lumber carriers completed after the war by the Albina Engine & Machine Works, Portland, Oregon, although under Maritime Commission designation. Powered by diesel machinery fitted aft, they had dimensions of 309 ft x 49 ft and a tonnage of 3,133 gross.

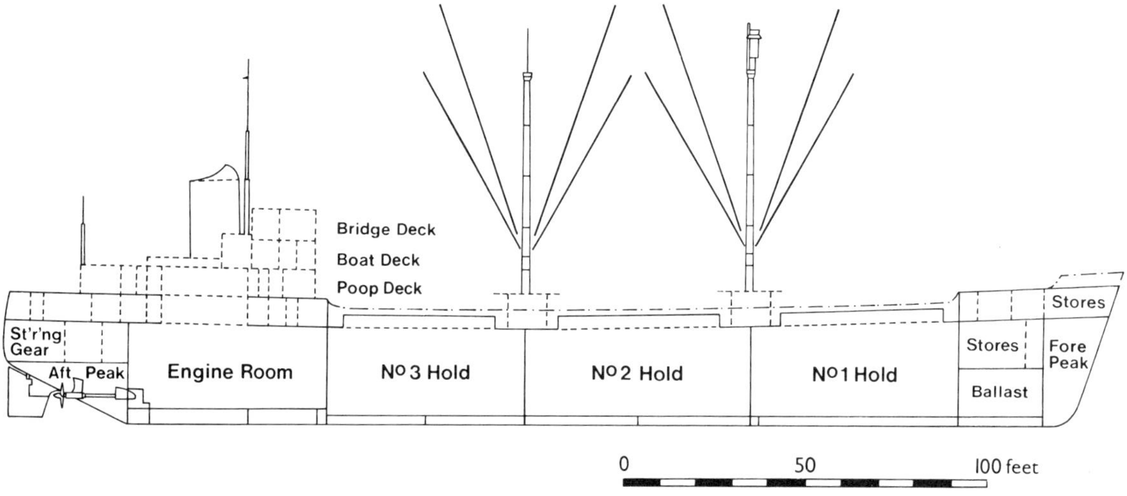

C1-MT-BU1 CARGO VESSEL

Only four were built and in 1947 three were acquired by Sword Line Inc. of New York, a company which, by the early 1950's had enhanced its fleet by the addition of further wartime tonnage including a T2 tanker and two Danish-built 'Hansa' type ships which, at the end of the war, had become 'Empire' ships under the British flag.

The remaining ship of the four passed to the Ponce Cement Corporation of New York, also in 1947. Later she went to the Mexican & West Indies SS Co (Isbrandtsen & Co) then to a subsidiary of Earl Smith & Co of New York, and later still to the Mexican Trader Corporation. Under this title she was lost in 1967. By this same year two from the Sword Line fleet had reverted to US government ownership and were ready for scrapping: the third vessel had been lost previously, in 1951.

MC Hull Nos 2530-2533 Yard Nos 215-218

215 OREGON FIR 11.45 1947: OREGON SWORD. 1967: Returned to US government. 1967: Scrapped USA.

216 CALIFORNIA REDWOOD 1.46 1947: CALIFORNIA SWORD. 1967: Returned to US government. 1967: Scrapped USA.

217 WASHINGTON CEDAR 3.46 1947: PONCE. 1958: MEXICAN TRADER. 1965: COSTA RICAN TRADER.

This ship was driven aground on 28 April 1967 close to cliffs inside rocky Bear Cove on the western side of the entrance to the harbour at Halifax, NS., by high winds and storm force seas. Her stern was so close to the shore that her crew put the ship's gangway across to nearby rocks and walked ashore after the gale had forced tugs to give up their salvage efforts. Next day more salvage attempts were abandoned when the ship broke in two and became a total loss. The following month work commenced on cutting up the ship for scrap.

Prior to her loss the vessel sustained severe ice damage when bound to Dalhousie from Comeau Bay. Towed to Halifax for repairs, she later left for Walton, NS., but only two hours later met her end in Bear Cove.

218 ARIZONA PINE 5.46 1947: ARIZONA SWORD.

On 5 May 1951 the ARIZONA SWORD was bound from New Orleans and New York for Portland, Maine, with a cargo of sulphur when she was in collision in the Cape Cod Canal with the Liberty type collier BERWINDVALE. The ARIZONA SWORD, severely damaged, was beached and abandoned, a CTL. Sold, she was refloated in May 1952 and towed to Boston. In 1954 she was converted to a barge by the Tampa Marine Co for coastwise service. This included removal of her propelling machinery, but she retained her name.

The P types

P1-S2-L2 type

The two ships of the US Navy's DOYEN class were small fast transports built by the Consolidated Steel Corporation at Los Angeles under Maritime Commission contracts. Given the names of Marine Corps Generals, the DOYEN and the FELAND formed part of the Navy's 1940 Fiscal Year programme.

They were laid down as transports with the intended designations of AP 2 and AP 18, respectively, each being designed to carry a battalion of the Marine Expeditionary Force which was maintained on both coasts of the USA in peacetime. Subsequently the ships were reclassed as Attack Transports and given the customary APA designation.

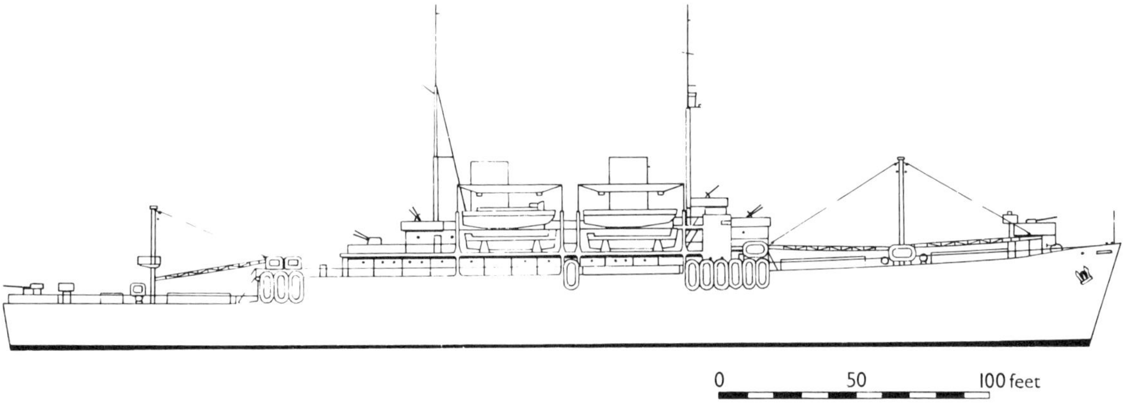

The troop transport FELAND

The outline of these two vessels was somewhat unusual, for they had two funnels of differing heights and two masts set close together — both on the midship structure, one forward and one aft — the latter being of the tripod type. The main deck was cut away at quarterdeck level and they were fitted aft with a ramp for the launching of small landing craft or for the unloading of tanks and heavy equipment. A number of landing craft were carried, these being nested amidships in special davits.

Propulsion machinery was twin geared turbines of 8,800 shp, driving twin screws and giving a speed of 19 knots.

Details:

Tonnages: 6710 gross
3000 nett
2150 deadweight
4351 displacement

Measurements: 411 ft 6 in length oa
385 ft 6 in length bp
56 ft breadth
34 ft depth
19 ft draught

MC Hull Nos 181-182 Yard Nos 206-207

U.S.S. DOYEN after trials in 1943 *Charles N. Dragonette collection*

206 DOYEN 3.43 Intended to be a transport (AP 2) for US Navy, but completed as an Attack Transport (APA 1) by Bethlehem Steel Corporation, San Pedro, Cal. 1946: To USMC Reserve. 1961: Loaned to Massachusetts Maritime Academy as a training ship, renamed BAY STATE. 1973: (Marad).

207 FELAND 6.43 Intended to be a transport (AP 18) for US Navy, but completed as an Attack Transport (APA 11). 1946: To USMC Reserve. 1964: Scrapped Portland, Ore.

U.S.S. DOYEN *U.S.N.*

P2 types

These P2 type ships were considered to be the biggest vessels built by the Maritime Commission during the war, for although they were somewhat shorter in length than the C5 type ore carriers their lightweight displacement was nearly double — at around 10,000 tons.

These large vessels were designed by the Commission in 1941, before the United States entered the war, under an instruction that the probable future need for troop transports would be the first priority. Yet, even at this early date, the Allied 'winning of the war' was accepted without question, for along with the instruction came another which ordered that the designs be made with postwar commercial operators in mind.

On 16 January 1942 a contract was awarded to the Federal SB Co at Kearny NJ, for ten vessels designated as the P2-S2-R2 type, and with it the thought that they might, later, be operated to South America by Moore McCormack or the Grace Lines. With this in mind the projected conversions for such service were provisionally designated as the P2-S2-R5 type but in the event these conversions were not carried out.

At the end of the same month ten more ships, this time designated as the P2-SE2-R1 type, were ordered from the Bethlehem Steel Co, who built a new yard at Alameda, California, for their construction. With this contract came the consideration that these ships might be operated, postwar, by the American President Lines to the Orient.

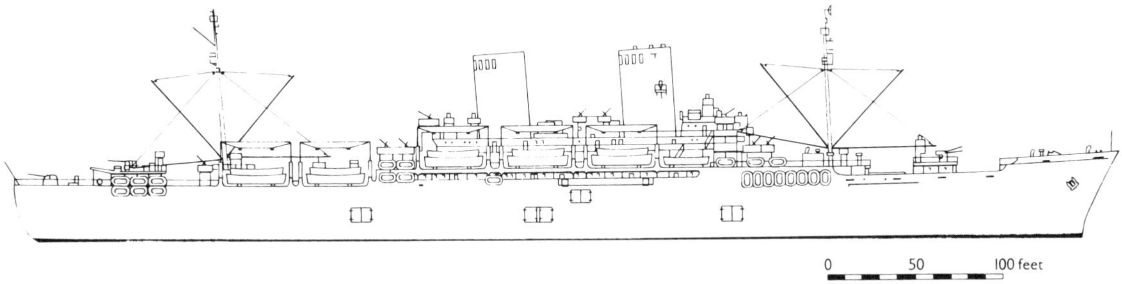

The troop transport GENERAL JOHN POPE

Accordingly, with these two differing routes in mind, the two types of ship were slightly different, the former being constructed with a 25 ft draught and a radius of some 12,000 miles whilst the latter had a draught of 29 ft and a 15,000 mile radius of action. Both types were propelled by turbines and twin screws, but whereas the Federal ships were fitted with C3 type geared turbines totalling 18,000 shp the Alameda-built ones were driven by turbo-electric drive of a thousand horsepower more. The differences in draught and horsepower balanced-out each other, for both types operated at some 19 knots. A constructional detail was that they were all built with separated engine rooms and thus twin funnels, this being considered essential for troopship safety but obviously somewhat uneconomical for commercial operation.

The first Federal P2 was delivered in July 1943 and by the end of the following year they had completed nine of their vessels, with the last one ready for delivery. With postwar operations in sight these builders were later awarded a contract for four more vessels. Only one of these was completed — in 1945. The remaining three, intended to be modified for the Atlantic service of the United States Lines and designated as the P2-S2-R4 type, were cancelled.

Also at the end of 1944 Bethlehem at Alameda had delivered three ships, had launched three more which were fitting out and had the remainder on the stocks. But by VJ day the last two ships were still under construction and the contracts were cancelled, work on the unfinished hulls being suspended. These incomplete hulls were later sold to American President Lines and were completed privately, being redesignated as the P2-SE2-R3 type, (see page 114).

The Federal-built P2 troop transports were all given 'General' names and in appearance were more powerful-looking than the Alameda ships — which were given 'Admiral' type names. There were two immediately-obvious differences between the classes: the former ships had slightly bigger funnels spaced somewhat closer together than those of their sisterships and, too, they had vertical ventilation slots cut in the aft face of the funnels. Also, they had two pole masts whereas the 'Admirals' carried two goalposts with fitted topmasts. With the 'Generals' the troop capacity was around 5,200 and cargo capacity around 100,000 cu ft. For the 'Admirals' the figures were 4,500/4,800 troops and between 36-48,000 cu ft, respectively.

One feature of particular interest was the air conditioning equipment installed, made necessary because the vessels were built without portholes for reasons of security. The equipment included 106 separate ventilating systems, these circulating 34 million cu ft of air per hour and requiring some 29 miles of piping.

All the ships comprising both these types were operated during the war by the US Navy, although mainly engaged in transporting Army personnel on Army schedules. However, whilst the 'Generals' (Army names) were operated by the Navy, the eight 'Admiral' vessels (suitably renamed in 1946) were operated for some time by the Army. Then, in October 1949, the MSTS took over all Navy and Army transport services and the eight ships again reverted to USN jurisdiction.

The non-commissioned ships of the MSTS (designated USNS — United States Navy Ship) — transports, cargo ships, tankers and the like — were identified by blue and gold bands on their funnels and with their names on bow and stern prefixed by the letters USNS. A prefix T to the ships pennant numbers also indicated assignment to the MSTS. In other respects they were painted as other USN ships. In 1955 the wartime armament was removed from active P2 ships.

GENERAL W. P. RICHARDSON as the liner LA GUARDIA, in 1950 *Skyfotos*

Previous to this, in 1946, many of the vessels were refitted for postwar operations, being given more comfortable accommodation for continued trooping service. Subsequently, one in particular (Federal yard No 276, the GENERAL W. P. RICHARDSON) became unique by being refitted and converted, and thus redesignated, four more times whilst still under American control. Later she was sold to Greek buyers and emerged from yet another conversion with extensive modernisation carried out both internally and externally. Less than two years later she was transferred to a cruise line operating out of Miami.

Similarly, over the years, there were some proposed conversions and redesignations for the eight Alameda-built vessels, the R6 design being intended for the American South African Line, the R7 for the Moore McCormack Lines and the R8 for American President Lines, but in the event none of the ships passed to commercial interests and these projects were cancelled.

Details:	R2 type	R1 type
Length oa	623 ft	609 ft
Length bp	573 ft	573 ft
Length waterline	590 ft	590 ft
Breadth, moulded	75 ft 6 in	75 ft 6 in
Depth, moulded	51 ft 6 in	43 ft 6 in
Tonnage, gross	17,951	17,001
Tonnage light displacement	11,450	12,650
Tonnage deadweight	8,200	8,750
Oil fuel, tons	3,046	3,936

P2-S2-R2 type

Built by Federal Shipbuilding & Drydock Co, Kearny, NJ.

MC Hull Nos 668-677	Yard Nos 268-277
2080	505
2081-2083	506-508 (cancelled August 1945)

268 GENERAL JOHN POPE 7.43 Completed for the US Navy as a transport (AP 110). 9.1946: Completed conversion by Bethlehem Steel Co, Hoboken, to post-war requirements for operation by US Army. 1950: Reverted to USN (T-AP 110). 1958: To Marad Reserve. 8.1965: Reacquired by USN. 1969: To Marad Reserve, Suisun Bay.

269 GENERAL ALEXANDER E. ANDERSON 8.43 Completed for the US Navy as a transport (AP 111). 6.1946: Completed conversion by Bethlehem Steel Co, Boston, to post-war requirements, renamed GENERAL A.E. ANDERSON. 1950: (T-AP 111). 1958: To Marad Reserve, Suisun Bay.

270 GENERAL WILLIAM A. MANN 10.43 Completed for the US Navy as a transport (AP 112). 1946: GENERAL W. A. MANN. 1950: (T-AP 112). 12.1966: To Marad Reserve, Hudson River. Later transferred to Reserve, James River.

GENERAL HENRY W. BUTNER as a troop transport *Tom Rayner*

271 GENERAL HENRY W. BUTNER 12.43 Completed for the US Navy as a transport (AP 113). 1946: GENERAL H. W. BUTNER. 1950: (T-AP 113). 3.1960: To Marad Reserve, James River.

On 25 January 1977 this vessel was towed from Reserve by the tug EVELYN COLLINS, bound for shipbreakers at Brownsville, Texas. Two days later, when some 27 miles from Oregon Inlet, N. Carolina, the tug had to release its tow due to heavy weather. Other vessels rendered assistance and the GENERAL BUTNER was towed to Norfolk, Va. Later she resumed her final voyage to the 'breakers yard, and was scrapped in September 1977.

272 GENERAL WILLIAM MITCHELL 1.44 Completed for the US Navy as a transport (AP 114). 1950: (T-AP 114). 12.1966: To Marad Reserve, Suisun Bay.

GENERAL GEORGE M. RANDALL off Los Angeles in March 1945 *U.S.M.C.*

273 GENERAL GEORGE M. RANDALL 4.44 Completed for the US Navy as a transport (AP 115). 1950: (T-AP 115). 1961: To Marad Reserve, James River. 6.1975: Sold to New York shipbreakers.

274 GENERAL M. C. MEIGS 6.44 Completed for the US Navy as a transport (AP 116). 1946: Transferred to US Army. Later scheduled for conversion and transfer to American President Lines (designation P2-S2-R12) but transaction cancelled. 1950: Reverted to USN (T-AP 116). 1958: To Marad Reserve, Olympia, Wash.

In January 1972 this ship — renamed MT 116 — was in tow of the tug GEAR, bound from the Navy yard at Bremerton for the Suisun Bay Reserve Fleet site. Lashed to her deck was a small naval tug, this for delivery at San Francisco.

On the morning of the 9th the ship broke loose from the tug in a gale and was driven ashore on the isolated rocky coast of the Makah Indian Reservation, near Portage Head, south of Cape Flattery. Pounded by heavy seas, the ship broke in two with her stern section impaled on jagged rocks. Continuing adverse weather soon caused the vessel to become a three-piece wreck and the small tug to become a total loss. The US Navy considered removing sections of the wrecked ship, but then postponed further action, believing any type of salvage to be uneconomic.

275 GENERAL W. H. GORDON 6.44 Completed for the US Navy as a transport (AP 117). 6.1946: Bareboat chartered to American President Lines (designation P2-S2-R10 type). Later transferred to US Army. 1951: Reverted to USN (T-AP 117). 1958: To Marad Reserve. 1961: Again reverted to USN (T-AP 117). 1968: To Marad Reserve, James River.

276 GENERAL W. P. RICHARDSON 10.44 Completed for the US Navy as a transport (AP 118). 5.1946: Completed conversion by Todd Shipyards, Hoboken, to postwar requirements for operation as a dependents/war brides ship by US Army (designation P2-S2-R7 type).

In 1949 the ship was acquired on bareboat charter by American Export Lines. Renamed LA GUARDIA and redesignated as the P2-S2-R10 type, she made her first commercial sailing — from New York for Genoa and Naples — in May 1949. Later her route was extended and amended to take in Gibraltar, Palermo, Piraeus and Haifa, but the service proved uneconomic and with the completion of the new liners INDEPENDENCE and CONSTITUTION in 1951 she became surplus to the company's needs. So, in December 1951 she was returned to Marad and reclassified as a troopship, in Reserve.

In 1955 a new company named Hawaiian SS Co (a subsidiary of Textron Inc) bid for, and secured the liner. Again refitted, she was renamed LEILANI, redesignated as the P2-S2-R12 type and emerged for service in the San Francisco-Honolulu trade with accommodation for 650 tourists. Again the service was not a success and in a short time her owners were bankrupt. Their backers defaulted on the mortgage and the ship was repossessed by Marad.

Her next buyers were American President Lines, in 1960. Sent for conversion to the Puget Sound Bridge & DD Co, Seattle, she emerged bearing little resemblance to the LEILANI.

The economy class accommodation for 658 passengers was reduced to 456 in first class, and other internal alterations included a new veranda built on the sun deck, a new dining room the full width of the ship and additional public rooms on the promenade deck. The most striking external change was the replacement of her original funnels by rakish, streamlined ones, the renewal of parts of the superstructure and the plating-in of the forward well deck. Under the name of PRESIDENT ROOSEVELT and designated as the P2-S2-R14a type, she made her first sailing, transpacific, in May 1962, joining her sisterships PRESIDENT WILSON and PRESIDENT CLEVELAND (see the P2-SE2-R3 type) on her owners fortnightly Far East service from San Francisco. These three vessels, with their light grey hulls, white superstructures and twin red, white and blue funnels sporting APL's 'eagle and stars' insignia thus became the most attractive trio afloat.

Early in 1970 the PRESIDENT ROOSEVELT was sold to Solon Nav. S.A. (the Chandris group), and in the May she went to Perama, near Piraeus, for a further refit, being renamed ATLANTIS. Little capital expenditure was involved so far as a shipyard was concerned, for the 'yard' was no more than an anchorage with a rented warehouse for a storeroom. Cabins aboard the ship were used as drawing offices, etc, and electric power was supplied by an old coaster, the CLEO, aided by thirty portable generators. This source of power gave a nett saving of about £1,000 per week. At the same time the BRITANIS (ex LURLINE, built in 1932) underwent a similar conversion and as a result Chandris, for an outlay of only some 20 million dollars (including the purchase prices) possessed two 20,000 ton liners in excellent condition and fully meeting American requirements for fire precautions — there being little wood left aboard. Laminated plastics were extensively used — thus enabling the ships to cruise from US ports.

The labour force at Perama consisted of about 700 men on board, with a similar number on shore engaged on prefabrication. Most of the work was sub-contracted, although the Chandris group had large shareholdings in the firms involved. A main advantage was that there was complete flexibility of labour, joiners, for example, doing most of the welding — thus saving around thirty per cent of the cost.

The refit of the ATLANTIS was completed in Rotterdam and she emerged in mid-1971 with another altered outline and extensive modernisation which included the use of 1,200 tons of steel. This included the addition of extra decks and a number of new public rooms. She became a one-class ship with accommodation for 1,092 passengers in 401 cabins, as opposed to her previous 456 passengers in 140 cabins.

Spring of 1971 saw her on the New York/Nassau run but in 1972 she was sold to Eastern Steamship Lines of Miami, with Chandris acquiring as part of the deal the cruise ship ARIADNE (6,644 grt). Under the flag of her new owners the vessel continued cruising in the USA/Caribbean service, being renamed EMERALD SEAS.

277 Laid down as GENERAL C. H. BARTH 12.44 Completed for the US Navy as a transport, renamed GENERAL WILLIAM WEIGEL (AP 119). 7.1946: Completed conversion by Todd Shipyards, Hoboken, to postwar requirements for operation by US Army. 1950: Reverted to USN (T-AP 119). 1958: To Marad Reserve. 8.1965: Reacquired by USN (T-AP 119). 1968: To Marad Reserve, Suisun Bay.

505 GENERAL J. C. BRECKINRIDGE 6.45 Completed for the US Navy as a transport (AP 176). 1950: (T-AP 176). 12.1966: To Marad Reserve, Suisun Bay.

506—507—508 Three vessels planned to slightly modified designs (intended to be of the P2-S2-R4 type) and intended for operation by the United States Lines as passenger ships on the North Atlantic route. Cancelled in August 1945, as their success in merchant service could not be guaranteed.

P2-SE2-R1 type

Built by Bethlehem-Alameda Shipyard Inc, Alameda, Cal, (later Bethlehem Steel Co, Shipbuilding Division, Alameda, Cal.)

MC Hull Nos 678-687 Yard Nos 9501-9510

9501 ADMIRAL W. S. BENSON 8.44 Completed for the US Navy as a transport (AP 120). 8.1946: Completed conversion by Bethlehem Steel Co, San Francisco, to postwar requirements for operation by US Army; renamed GENERAL DANIEL I. SULTAN. 1950: Reverted to USN (T-AP 120) (same name). 11.1968: To Marad Reserve, Suisun Bay.

9502 ADMIRAL W. L. CAPPS 9.44 Completed for the US Navy as a transport (AP 121). 8.1946: Completed conversion by Todd Shipyards, Hoboken, to postwar requirements for operation by US Army; renamed GENERAL HUGH L. GAFFEY. 1950: Reverted to USN (T-AP 121) (same name). 11.1968: To Marad Reserve, Suisun Bay.

ADMIRAL R. E. COONTZ as GENERAL ALEXANDER M. PATCH *Author's collection*

9503 ADMIRAL R. E. COONTZ 11.44 Completed for the US Navy as a transport (AP 122). 6.1946: Completed conversion by Bethlehem Steel Co, New York, to postwar requirements for operation by US Army; renamed GENERAL ALEXANDER M. PATCH. 1950: Reverted to USN (T-AP 122) (same name). 5.1970: To Marad Reserve, James River.

9504 ADMIRAL E. W. EBERLE 1.45 Completed for the US Navy as a transport (AP 123). 8.1946: Completed conversion by Todd Shipyards, Los Angeles, to postwar requirements for operation by US Army; renamed GENERAL SIMON B. BUCKNER. 1950: Reverted to USN (T-AP 123) (same name). 3.1970: To Marad Reserve, James River.

9505 ADMIRAL C. F. HUGHES 1.45 Completed for the US Navy as a transport (AP 124). 7.1946: Completed conversion by Bethlehem Steel Co, San Francisco, to postwar requirements for operation by US Army; renamed GENERAL EDWIN D. PATRICK. 1950: Reverted to USN (T-AP 124) (same name). 9.1968: To Marad Reserve, Suisun Bay.

9506 ADMIRAL H. T. MAYO 4.45 Completed for the US Navy as a transport (AP 125). 7.1946: Completed conversion by Todd Shipyards, Brooklyn, to postwar requirements for operation by US Army; renamed GENERAL NELSON M. WALKER. 1950: Reverted to USN (T-AP 125) (same name). 1958: To Marad Reserve, but reacquired by USN again almost immediately as a result of the Lebanon landings of July 1958. 1.1959: To Marad Reserve. 9.1965: Again to USN (T-AP 125). 4.1970: To Marad Reserve, James River.

ADMIRAL HUGH RODMAN as the transport GENERAL MAURICE ROSE *Skyfotos*

9507 ADMIRAL HUGH RODMAN 7.45 Completed for the US Navy as a transport (AP 126). 8.1946: Completed conversion by Bethlehem Steel Co, New York, to postwar requirements for operation by US Army; renamed GENERAL MAURICE ROSE. 1950: Reverted to USN (T-AP 126) (same name). 6.1970: To Marad Reserve, James River.

ADMIRAL W. S. SIMS as GENERAL WILLIAM O. DARBY *World Ship Photo Library*

9508 ADMIRAL W. S. SIMS 9.45 Completed for the US Navy as a transport (AP 127). 8.1946: Completed conversion by Bethlehem Steel Co, San Pedro, to postwar requirements for operation by US Army; renamed GENERAL WILLIAM O. DARBY. 1950: Reverted to USN (T-AP 127) (same name). 6.1970: To Marad Reserve, James River.

9509 ADMIRAL D. W. TAYLOR See P2-SE2-R3 type.

9510 ADMIRAL F. B. UPHAM See P2-SE2-R3 type.

P2-SE2-R3 type

The two vessels which became the PRESIDENT CLEVELAND and the PRESIDENT WILSON were laid down in 1944 as Navy transports of the P2-SE2-R1 type.

Cancelled by the USMC at the end of the war whilst still incomplete, the hulls were purchased by the American President Lines and redesigned as luxury liners, being designated as the R3 type. They were for their premier trans-pacific California-Orient express service — which was operated before the war by the PRESIDENT HOOVER, lost on a reef off Japan in December 1937 and the PRESIDENT COOLIDGE, sunk by a mine in the Pacific whilst serving as a US transport.

PRESIDENT CLEVELAND, laid down as ADMIRAL D. W. TAYLOR *Author's collection*

The hulls of the two R3 ships were of combined rivetted/welded construction, with a curved stem, a cruiser stern and with three complete decks and an additional partial deck. Above these was the upper deck which extended from stem almost to the stern, a promenade deck, a boat deck and a bridge deck. The midship house above the boat deck was of rivetted aluminium, this saving some 75 tons weight in the superstructure. Up to this time aluminium had been used only rarely in merchant ship construction, although the US Navy had used it on the superstructures of destroyers and cruisers with very satisfactory results.

Accommodation on the liners was provided for 552 passengers in both cabin and tourist classes. Among the facilities for their comfort were two swimming pools, libraries, a cinema, massage rooms, beauty parlours and barber shops and a gymnasium. Kennels were fitted for the carriage of dogs. The crew of each vessel totalled 338 persons.

Interesting cargo handling gear was the side port loading/discharging crane for No 4 hatch, which topped out on A deck. With this crane two bridges each carrying a trolley capable of handling $2\frac{1}{2}$ tons were installed for athwartship travel. Thirteeen refrigerated cargo compartments in each ship totalled over 52,000 cu ft, whilst their own domestic compartments were an additional 18,000 cu ft.

The military philosophy of the original design of the ships was reflected in the propulsion machinery, there being complete separation of the two power plant units and the two motor units. Each power unit comprised two boilers, each generating 40,000 pounds of steam per hour. This steam was led to the unit's turbo-generator set, which in turn supplied current to the electric propulsion motors. Each of these had the normal 9,000 shp rating of the P2 type ships, giving a cruising speed of 19 knots.

After serving American President Lines for some 25 years both vessels were sold in 1973 to C.Y. Tung of Hong Kong and placed under the flag of the associated Oceanic Cruises Development Inc, carrying the owners customary 'Oriental' prefix to their new names.

Later in the same year the ORIENTAL EMPRESS (cx PRESIDENT WILSON) called at Colombo in the course of a 100 day world cruise and became the first of the big liners to call since tourist traffic became negligible after the 1967 closure of the Suez Canal. With the tourist trade beginning to regain some importance, she was followed by the French liner FRANCE, though a call by the P & O liner CANBERRA was cut due to a then world-wide fuel shortage. This same shortage also caused the abandonment of the next projected round-the-world cruise of the ORIENTAL EMPRESS and in early 1974 the ship was laid up at Hong Kong. Later, she re-entered service, but was again laid up in September 1975.

The ORIENTAL PRESIDENT (ex PRESIDENT CLEVELAND) also arrived at Hong Kong — in March 1974 — but she was soon sold to shipbreakers, arriving at Kaohsiung in June 1974 for scrapping.

Details:

Tonnages: 15,456 gross
10,224 deadweight
22,574 full displacement
12,350 light displacement
Oil fuel 4,422 tons
Cruising range 17,600 miles

Measurements: 619 ft 6 in length oa
573 ft length bp
75 ft 6 in breadth
52 ft 6 in depth to upper deck
30 ft draught

Built by Bethlehem-Alameda Shipyard Inc., Alameda, Cal (later Bethlehem Steel Co, Shipbuilding Division, Alameda, Cal.)

MC Hull Nos 686-687 Yard Nos 9509-9510

9509 Laid down as ADMIRAL D. W. TAYLOR 12.47 Laid down in August 1944 and launched June 1946. Intended to be completed as a US Navy transport (AP 128) but contract cancelled. Incomplete hull sold and completed privately as PRESIDENT CLEVELAND. 1973: ORIENTAL PRESIDENT. 6.1974: Arrived Kaohsiung for scrapping.

PRESIDENT WILSON as ORIENTAL EMPRESS *Michael Lennon*

9510 Laid down as ADMIRAL F. B. UPHAM 4.48 Launched in November 1946. Intended to be completed as a US Navy transport (AP 129) but contract cancelled. Incomplete hull sold and completed privately as PRESIDENT WILSON. 1973: ORIENTAL EMPRESS.

P2-S1-DN3 type

On three dates during 1949, these being 1 June, 1 August and 30 September, three round-the-world liners — then designated as the P2-S1-DN1 type — were laid down for the American President Lines by the New York SB Co, Camden, NJ.

The first, PRESIDENT JACKSON, was launched in June 1950 and scheduled for delivery in the December. The PRESIDENT ADAMS and the PRESIDENT HAYES were to be launched — with a two month interval — in August and October 1950, respectively. Four more similar ships were envisaged, thereby ultimately permitting the company to offer a sailing in the service every two weeks. The ships were to carry 204 first class passengers and would call at thirty ports in seventeen countries during each voyage.

Following the outbreak of war in Korea it was announced by Marad on 16 September 1950 that these three ships — and the liner UNITED STATES — would be taken over and completed as troop transports for the US Navy. As a result, the completion of the PRESIDENT JACKSON, which had previously been expedited to December 1950 for a scheduled maiden voyage in January 1951, was cancelled. Actually she was not completed until twelve months later, being renamed BARRETT. The PRESIDENT ADAMS, now renamed GEIGER, was finally launched in October 1950 and the PRESIDENT HAYES, as UPSHUR, in January 1951, with their completion dates as transports extending to September and December 1952, respectively.

The Navy transport UPSHUR, laid down as PRESIDENT HAYES *Skyfotos*

The ships were redesignated as the P2-S1-DN3 type.

They were equipped with spacious berthing areas and comfortable messing and recreational facilities to the highest post-war standards. Passenger capacity of each was 1,500 troops plus 396 cabin berths for officers and dependents. In an emergency the troop capacity could be quickly increased by over a thousand by conversion of the recreation areas to berthing spaces.

The outstanding point of the ships' profiles showed a dummy funnel combined with and faired into the bridge superstructure, with twin funnels abaft this somewhat resembling kingposts.

Later American President Lines considered construction of three improved versions to replace the vessels, but in 1955 they acquired replacement ships in the form of three of Marad's post-war 'Mariner' type ships.

Details:

Tonnages: 13,319 gross
7,158 nett
6,898 deadweight
17,600 displacement
Turbines: 13,750 shp
Speed 19–20 knots

Measurements: 503 ft 3 in length (regstd)
499 ft 6 in length (moulded)
73 ft breadth
49 ft depth

MC Hull Nos 2914-2916 Yard Nos 485-487

485 Laid down as PRESIDENT JACKSON (II) 12.51 Taken over by the US Navy and completed as a transport, renamed BARRETT (T-AP 196). 3.1973: (Marad). 9.1973: Reactivated at Oakland, Cal., and transferred to the New York Maritime College for use as a training ship. Renamed EMPIRE STATE V. Later renamed EMPIRE STATE.

GEIGER, a U.S. Navy transport, in 1956 *John G. Callis*

486 Laid down as PRESIDENT ADAMS (II) 9.52 Taken over by the US Navy and completed as a transport, renamed GEIGER (T-AP 197). 4.1971: (Marad). In Reserve, Suisun Bay.

487 Laid down as PRESIDENT HAYES (II) 12.52 Taken over by the US Navy and completed as a transport, renamed UPSHUR (T-AP 198). 3.1973: Withdrawn from military service, transferred to Maine Maritime Academy for use as a training ship. Renamed STATE OF MAINE.

UPSHUR as STATE OF MAINE, in 1978 *Wright & Logan*

These three vessels operated originally under the auspices of the Military Sea Transportation Service and this continued when that body became the Military Sealift Command. The Command covered four main areas, designated as Far East, Atlantic, East Atlantic/Mediterranean and Pacific. The year of 1973 saw a sudden reduction in MSC ship totals and the withdrawal of two of these DN3 type ships. At the beginning of the year 221 ships were controlled, but at years'end the fleet had declined by 69 vessels.

The Vietnam conflict maintained MSC activity, but the withdrawal of US forces led to ultimate reduction to a point where — by 1975 — expenditure was less than half of the 1969 figure.

In sixty days following the ceasefire MSC Far East lifted 227,000 tons of cargo from Vietnam during operation 'Roll Up' which required the lift of valuable military equipment involving ships ranging from LST's to heavy lift vessels of the C4 type.

In the same year violence in the Middle East generated more Sealift requirements, these being met by MSC and Navy ships and by commercial tankers and cargo carriers, the latter carrying 94% of all military cargo during the year.

During the same period MSC Pacific also changed. In the March the troop transports BARRETT and UPSHUR returned to Oakland after having made their last passenger trips transporting Korean combat divisions back to Pusan from Vietnam. The BARRETT went to Reserve, but soon became a school ship. The UPSHUR followed for similar use. Other withdrawals included refrigerated store ships, cargo ships and special project ships and the replacement of C1-M's on expensive Pacific Islands services with a fast chartered vessel. An addition, from the Atlantic fleet, was the converted S4 type cable ship AEOLUS, whilst the similar THOR was placed in 'ready reserve' status at Oakland. By this time the remaining DN3 type trooper, the GEIGER, was in Reserve at Suisun Bay.

PART ONE INDEX OF ORIGINAL AND COMPLETION NAMES

The prefix (I), (II) etc means first or second ship so named within the whole range of the United States Maritime Commission programme.